BOOKS BY CARLETON BEALS:

HOUSE IN MEXICO
TASTE OF GLORY
ADVENTURE OF THE WESTERN SEA
MEXICAN MAZE (Book Club of America)
DAWN OVER THE AMAZON
       (Literary Guild. *Liberty* reprint)
PORFIRIO DIAZ: Dictator of Mexico
        (Guggenheim Fellowship)
THE COMING STRUGGLE FOR LATIN AMERICA
    (*Readers' Digest* condensation. Halcyon reprint)
MEXICO: An Interpretation
STEPHEN F. AUSTIN: Father of Texas
CHILE: The Long Land
LANDS OF THE DAWNING MORROW
RIO GRANDE TO CAPE HORN
PANAMERICA: A Program for the Western Hemisphere
AMERICA SOUTH
FIRE ON THE ANDES
THE CRIME OF CUBA
BANANA GOLD
THE STONES AWAKE
BLACK RIVER
DESTROYING VICTOR
OUR YANKEE HERITAGE: New England
      Contributions to American Civilization
OUR YANKEE HERITAGE: The Making of Bristol
OUR YANKEE HERITAGE: The Making of New Haven
THE STORY OF HUEY LONG
AMERICAN EARTH: The Biography of a Nation
BRIMSTONE AND CHILI
THE GREAT CIRCLE
GLASS HOUSES
ROME OR DEATH: The Story of Fascism

House in Mexico

House in Mexico

BY

CARLETON BEALS

WITH DRAWINGS BY

TOM O'SULLIVAN

HASTINGS HOUSE, PUBLISHERS,   NEW YORK

Published simultaneously in Canada
by S. J. Reginald Saunders, Publishers,
Toronto 2B.

Library of Congress Catalog Card Number: 58–9007

Printed in the United States of America

Parts of several chapters have been printed in
THE NEW YORKER, VIRGINIA QUARTERLY and STAG.

CONTENTS

CONTENTS

House in Mexico

I

HOUSE IN COYOACÁN

IT was seven in the morning, and the church bells were ringing again. A finger of sunlight poked along the floor and struck fire in the rainbow sarape. In the patio, velvet shadows caressed the white calla lilies. The sun grew on the interlaced brick balustrade, and a softer echo of light lay on the high pink inner wall that shut off the neighboring house. From it came the stirring radio strains of "Anchors Aweigh," followed by oompety-oomp setting-up exercises.

Chubby Mario, sweeping the red entrance tiles with a long twig broom, was raising a cloud of dust. His yesterday's snowy communion suit was now badly soiled. In the kitchen, his mother, brown weazened Petra, was fanning the charcoal fire beneath an olla of coffee. José, her husband, was busy sprinkling the cabbage and bean sprouts, bursting through the soil to meet the upland violet rays. María was already scrubbing clothes in the concrete tubs in the back corral. Guadalupe was combing her long black hair on the brick stoop. Her pretty grape eyes were swollen from weeping over a faithless chauffeur. She rose with a deep sigh and a queenly air to scrub the yellow pine floors with soap and zacate fiber. It was quite a menage for a writer who had sought out this quiet spot in Mexico for cheap living and independence.

I had fallen in love with the house the minute I laid eyes on it, one of a row of blue and pink flat-roofed dwellings on cobbled, grass-grown Ave María Street in the ancient village of Coyoacán. They faced a fifteen-foot stone wall with mossy colonial buttresses sticking well into the street and overtowered by spruces, eucalyptus, and giant ahuehuete trees.

The little street butted into the gold-brown front of El Morenito—The Little Brown One—a flyspecked cubbyhole store, then jogged to become a cart track meandering off among little adobe houses and flowering gardens behind fat organ-cactus fences. Presently the track narrowed to a path that lost itself among the boulders of a gully fringing the Pedregal, a prehistoric chaotic lava flow stretching for many miles toward purple Ajusco Volcano to the south.

The Ave María neighborhood, with its dilapidated walls, rambling vines, and massed flowers, had the general hazy air of an eighteenth-century French romantic painting, but was warmer in color, more biblical in composition. Over this street, as over all Coyoacán, had drifted the soft mist of time, the melancholy of antiquity and semi-abandon. That was before the big postwar boom.

A yellowed newspaper tied to the iron-grilled balcony of the house had informed me it was for rent, and I lifted the iron knocker, shaped like a little hand. A dumpy gnarled Indian woman swung the massive double door open with a generous gesture, her wrinkled walnut face wreathed in a shy, mysterious smile. On her brick-colored plaid blouse, a rooster brooch of glass diamonds and rubies caught the afternoon sun with a glitter of magnificence.

She pattered ahead of me over the red tiles, her straight black hair slapping her back, her multiple wide skirts swishing in a surf of rose and green, blue and yellow.

The patio was beaten into hard earth, no garden at all, but a clump of ivy glistened in one corner, and red trumpet vines, honeysuckle, and bougainvillaea hung in dense masses of color and perfume over the encircling wall. A raised-tile-roofed corridor ran in an ell about two sides of the patio and onto it opened the double glass French doors of five gigantic calcimined rooms. The tiled kitchen had built-in charcoal braziers. The bathroom had no tub, only a homemade concrete toilet that worked well, concrete floor, and pipes for a shower. On a brick pedestal in the back corral stood a strange charcoal water-heating contraption and tank. Water was provided by an artesian well with an electric motor.

I signed the lease with two pious elderly French-Mexican spinsters who owned a lovely colonial mansion, surrounded by vast rambling gardens and orchards beyond the massive buttressed wall across the street. They begged me to enjoy their garden. "Whenever you are in the mood come and read or bring your typewriter, and we'll have a table set up on the terrace or under the trees. No one will disturb you."

Petra, who seemed to be an inseparable part of the house I had rented, set to work at once to scrub all the floors and sweep the lofty ceilings with turkey feathers on the end of a twelve-foot bamboo pole. She lived in an adobe shack around the corner.

"Will you get breakfast for me, Petra? And clean house once a week?"

"*Pues sí,* señor—with much pleasure—although I have never hired out for such duty—only to scrub and work of that sort." "Travail of that category," she actually said—those magniloquent Latin words that always flow out of humble Indian lips as naturally and melodiously as water.

"But you can cook?"

"A wee bit, señor." Her solemn, determined face flowered into a warm smile.

"But perhaps not the way the Señor is accustomed to."

"We can fix that. How much do you want?"

"Whatever the Señor is pleased to give me."

"Let us say twelve pesos a month."

She clasped her hands unbelievingly. "In Coyoacán, señor, the pay is only eight pesos a month, and that is for everything and for all day. For such a sum I shall cook all your meals and wash and mend your clothes."

"Where do you come from, Petra? You do not seem like the people in the city."

"I am from the *tierra caliente*—the hot country—below Cuautla. It is beautiful there and people are honest. City folk are corrupted, but for one who owns no land it is easier to make a living in these parts."

Petra took over completely. The house was scrubbed from top to bottom daily, breakfast was never late. Other meals, although she prepared only Mexican dishes, were marvelous and abundant.

To furnish such baronial rooms, which seemed to call for

the massive furniture of colonial times, presented a problem. I bought native stuff, plain tables and cabinets which I painted, and low Cuernavaca reed chairs with bird and animal designs flitting over their lacquered red-and-green backs. An old mahogany desk of massive proportions cost me only ten dollars. I puttied up the termite holes and polished it. Later I sold it for one hundred dollars. Artist friends loaned me pictures and drawings. For blankets, rugs, and hangings I used Texcoco and Oaxaca textiles I planned to keep. For a few pesos Petra bought a large assortment of terra-cotta bowls, pots, and dishes.

Every morning, when the shadows were still long and soft, I went out to the back corral in pajamas and robe and took a splash at the overflow tank. Small quail sipped at the rivulets, even perched on the edge of the tank beside me, busily bathing and fluffing their feathers. When my own snorting grew too obstreperous, they would fly away a few feet and look at me reproachfully.

I was lathered with soap when Petra came running out. *"Buenos días,"* she greeted me gravely, with no hint of embarrassment. Getting a dishcloth from the line, she swished back inside before I could even grab for my robe. Whenever she found it necessary to come to the back patio, my bathing never gave her pause; she came and went as she pleased.

Otherwise I had full privacy behind the high walls. Petra always left after lunch for several hours, and I would spread out a mat in the corral or the patio and take sun baths. But one afternoon giggling and chattering woke me from my siesta. Two servant girls next door had rigged up a clothesline on the flat roof of an adjoining storage shed and were hanging out washing.

"Buenos días," they said in a friendly way, on seeing that

I was awake, and went on with their task and their chatter as though it were quite usual to see a naked man flat on his back in the sun.

My Puritan upbringing had always confused morality with clothes. I tried nonchalantly to smoke a cigarette, but soon fled into the house.

One noon, glancing out of the rear bathroom window through the iron reja, I was startled to see a girl squatting stark naked on top of my concrete washtubs. She was lathering herself all over vigorously and shampooing her black hair. She was, I judged, about sixteen, dark-skinned, flat-chested, with little bowed chicken legs. Beside her lay a pile of freshly washed clothes ready to hang on the line.

At lunch I asked Petra about the apparition. "Who is the girl who takes a bath like a roosting pigeon on the edge of the scrubbing tubs?"

"That is my daughter, María. She is helping me with the washing."

One morning when I went out for my dip María was already scrubbing clothes again. I cleared my throat, "María, I'm going to take my bath."

"*Pues sí,* señor, *como no*—why not?" she answered indifferently, and pounded a shirt.

"But would you mind going into the patio or the kitchen?"

She rubbed her stringy black hair out of her eyes with one soapy arm and looked at me with astonishment. Then she fled giggling.

A few mornings later the same encounter occurred. "María, I'm going to take my bath."

"Go right ahead, señor." She kept on pounding clothes.

"But . . ."

"Señor, I have to get this washing done, for I must go to

town early. Don't mind me." She kept on scrubbing.

As I rubbed myself to a glow I considered the setup. I had hired Petra, but obviously María was now part of my establishment. Little by little she not only washed clothes, but scrubbed, made beds, helped cook, waited on table, yet Petra had asked me for no extra money for wages or food.

About a week later a chubby boy of ten was busily sweeping the front patio as I went for my bath.

"Hello there!"

"*Buenos días*, señor." A shy grin spread over his brown moon face.

"And who is the well-set-up young gentleman sweeping the tiles?" I asked Petra at breakfast.

"That is Mario, my son. I was late, so I had him sweep out. Also he will scrub the swallow droppings off the entrance tiles." She frowned. "What pests! I shall knock their nests down."

I explained that I loved those swallows. Every English manor house has nesting swallows. They are there in Shakespeare. They chirp through all the romantic love scenes in literature. I had never hoped to have swallows.

Petra mumbled, and her movements became jerky as always when something did not please her. The next day the swallows were ruthlessly ejected.

From then on every morning I woke to the swish of Mario's homemade twig broom in the patio. Usually he wore raggedy blue overalls, but when he began waiting on table, if there were guests, he always put on his white communion suit with a wide red sash. On occasions this garb was spotless. He took his new duty most seriously, but he could rarely keep his chubby thumb out of the soup. So he, too, became part and parcel of my household.

It was time to spade up for a garden. Petra watched me peck at the hard-packed ground. "I shall get you a good gardener, señor."

"I can't afford one. Besides, I need the exercise."

But when I returned from the city late that afternoon a stocky little brown man with a drooping stringy mustache was hard at work. Already he had turned over most of the back patio, an enormous place, had raked it down fine, and had divided it into artistic plots and paths. Half of the front patio had also been spaded.

"*Buenos días,* my friend. That looks fine. How much do you earn?"

"This is not for pay, señor, but because my woman asked me to do it."

"I see. But how much is such work worth ordinarily?"

"Señor, the usual pay is a peso a day, though a real gardener might get a bit more."

I gave him a peso and a quarter and told him I would finish it myself.

"As the Señor wishes," he answered politely. Wrinkling his nose thoughtfully, he continued, "We shall need a sprinkling can, a trowel, and seeds. If the Señor will give me the money, I will get everything this afternoon. Two pesos will be ample. In fact"—he grinned—"I could buy a drink of pulque as well, if the Señor would not be put out."

"With my compliments, only buy the things before you buy the pulque."

I asked Petra who our gardener was.

"My husband, Don José."

"I have paid him off and will finish the garden myself."

"Surely, señor. But it was not for pay he came."

"Is he the father of Mario and María?"

"No, señor. Their father is dead."

The following morning my work at the typewriter went fine, and it was high noon before I paused for a cigarette on the patio corridor. There was José working fertilizer into the beds. He dashed to the back corral to fill his shiny new sprinkling can.

"*Buenos días,* Don José. Things are certainly going to grow well."

"It will be a good season, God willing."

Later I scolded Petra. "I said . . ."

"But he loves to garden, señor. It was you who mentioned pay. He doesn't expect anything. His meals maybe? The money you allow me is sufficient."

It occurred to me that the incredibly small amount she had asked from me for food had been sufficient for quite some time. "Of course," I said. "But why does she want to work here for nothing?"

"He is my husband, Señor, and while he has no job, he will tend your garden. Don't bother your head about it a second longer."

José knew much about plants. I asked about insecticides.

"In the hot country the *bichos*—the insects—devour everything, but here where it is high the sun kills them off. All we need is a little nicotine solution for the roses, and that I can make from your cigarette stubs."

He was right: the violet rays at this high altitude not only killed insects and fungi, it caused the vegetables to grow more rapidly than in a Walt Disney film. In a few weeks the radishes were as big as golf balls, yet crisp and tender all the way through, so were the oversized beets and carrots.

One morning I came upon another girl busily ironing my clothes. "Hello! Lending Petra a hand?"

"*Si*, Señor, while I can, and God willing."

She lifted a coquettish shoulder, pulling her short yellow rayon dress above the red bow of her garter. She had a neat ankle and knew it—plenty of "salt," as they say here.

"Guadalupe is my other daughter," Petra told me. "She has been working in the arms factory."

I soon suspected that the only arms factory she had worked in was that of the worthless chauffeur with whom she had run off. He had tossed her back. For days she had wept bitterly, then snapped her big black eyes coquettishly again.

"She will help me while she may," Petra said.

"And pray tell," I asked, with belated apprehension, "just how many children have you?"

"Only the three, señor. God blessed me with no more."

"And how many other relatives have you?"

She began muttering names and counting on her fingers. By the time she had covered the fingers of both hands and was starting over again, I saw visions of being overrun with new faces and willing hands.

She gave off counting and sighed. "There are too many to count, señor."

I choked on the water I was drinking. "And of course you love every one of them and want them near you."

"Most certainly, señor. For most I would do anything."

"Very commendable," I murmured, wondering if I hadn't better begin planning a trip around the world.

"They all live in Cuautla and can rarely afford to come to the city," she continued. "Nor would they be happy here. They don't even write me, for the *escribanos*, the public letter writers, charge aplenty."

Apparently—and God willing—my establishment had absorbed its full quota. Enthusiastically I said, "All your youngsters are nice kids, Petra."

"Lupe gives me headaches. But she's so pretty, what else can you expect?"

So I came to have five kindly humans at my beck and call, apparently asking nothing from life but to serve me with alacrity. Happy, frequently singing, always interested in whatever they were doing, they injected surprising drama into the simplest tasks. For no good reason, except perhaps to change the routine, they would go to the extra trouble of taking the dirty dishes to the corral to wash them. Such little variations in time, place, and method converted the necessary tasks into novelty. Nor did they consider anything I requested unreasonable, but always flew to tend to it.

This shiny, clear morning before I stirred from my bed they were already busy about the place. I listened to the last of my neighbor's radio oompety-oomp exercises. The church bells started up again, no slow, sonorous pealing as in northern climes, but impatient tomtom strokes—"Get up! Get up! Get up!" gleeful, commanding, slightly barbaric.

The heavy pound came from big San Juan Bautista. Santa Catalina chimed in higher-pitched but softer. Then, faintly, mellow San Antonio de Padua. From across the Pedregal came the distant call, now full on the breeze, now dying away, of the little church in the tiny thatched village almost hidden in the higgledy-piggledy lava among cactus and false pepper trees.

After my bath hot coffee was steaming ready. For the sixteenth time I showed Petra exactly how to set the table.

"Is it really so important," she asked, "always to put the spoons and forks on exactly the same way? A spoon is a spoon wherever it lies."

"Perhaps you had better let María do it. She knows how and sometimes acts on what she knows. You really do find it amusing, don't you, Petra?"

She shrugged. "Señor, you are *gente de razón*—a reasoning person—and we are not."

It was the customary Indian description recognizing the difference between upper-class and foreign cultures and their own more intuitive sensitive way of life—different but not necessarily inferior except materially. Belonging to a long-subjugated society, the Indian finds his greatest sense of security in tenacious cultural and racial solidarity.

By some miracle the money I allowed Petra for food and laundry soap was still sufficient to feed her whole tribe without cutting down on the quality and quantity of my own meals. Whatever was left, if any, the others ate. Some dishes she prepared for me were not liked by them. Their chief delight was a well-seasoned plate of beans, and no other people on the globe can prepare them in a more savory and digestible form. A big olla of beans always simmered over the charcoal day and night. By the end of the week they were ambrosia.

Every so often I slipped José, who continued to tend to the garden and perform other duties, a peso, which he spent mostly on pulque. When some vendor came to the door, and Petra or the girls looked at a ribbon or trinket longingly, I made them buy it. This required much urging, but the glow on their faces was worth a thousand times the paltry sum.

Mario had his wiles. He would appear at my door, twisting his sombrero and grinning. "Perhaps there is something *special* today the Señor would like me to do after school?" At the slightest hint, he would fly to do anything, any and every errand. But something *special*, a suggestion he made only at rare intervals, meant he would get paid something.

"You can leave this note at the Calderóns'. Don't get it dirty." I gave him ten centavos.

His round face lit up like daybreak and he dashed off with a grimace of triumph for his older sisters.

"You folks do everything nicely," I told Petra.

"The Señor is so good to us, so we are happy. Please tell us whenever anything is not to your liking."

"Only one thing. Please don't let Lupe scrub the floors every day. It is too much work, and it makes the house damp in the mornings. Once a week will be plenty."

"But señor . . ." She flounced off, muttering darkly. In fact, any suggestion they do less work always seemed to make them unhappy.

If a trifle set in her ways, Petra had no recognizable faults, never a harsh word for anybody, not even her children, although they obeyed her always and promptly without the slightest argument. No member of the nobility ever had finer manners or such consideration for others.

Her one besetting sin in my eyes was that she was a plate snatcher. She had the sound peasant notion that food was to be put down the gullet without delay. If anybody stopped to converse, lo! on looking down again there would be no food before him. I implored her not to be so hasty. It did no good. I told her never to take a course off till I gave her the sign. It did no good. Finally I bought a small bell and sternly forbade her to remove anything from the table until I rang it. That worked.

"The bell was a pretty good idea, wasn't it, Petra?"

She sniffed and flounced. "Bells are for cows!"

The days flowed rhythmically through the rainy months. Every afternoon torrents fell briefly, hammering on the pave-

ment, the heavy drops prancing like white-skirted ballet
dancers. For a short while it would drive down so hard it
blotted out the pink wall beside the patio. Mornings were
always singing with sunshine and silken skies, but about two
every afternoon a cauliflower puff of cloud grew on the horizon, soon white suds churned, in a few minutes an army of
black clouds marched across the sky. Suddenly a terrific gust
of wind, then dead calm, then the heavens burst apart. With
the downpour came a swift drop in temperature, sometimes
thirty degrees or more in a short space of time, a sudden
drain on the body's energies that induced lassitude and
pleasing melancholy. But after fifteen minutes or half an hour
the rain eased off to a drizzle. Then the sky cleared. After a
few last-minute April-like showers the world would become
fresh and glistening, and, no matter how hot the day, the
mugginess never returned. The day stayed coolish until the
chill of the highland night. On rare occasions the rain lasted
till sunset, then the cloud colorings were stunning, a band
of apple-green around the horizon, topped by fleecy lilacs,
pinks, and lavenders.

Early those zestful mornings of sharp-cut shadows and
sounds, sweetly shrill because of the rarefied atmosphere, I
strolled through the town. It was an aloof half-Indian community, none of the showy trappings like San Angel, but
centuries older than Mexico City, which was first settled in
1325. Prehistoric codices show Coyoacán captured by the
Aztecs during their long pillar-to-post migrations well before
they became powerful enough to dominate the entire valley
of Mexico and found their capital in the Texcoco marshes.
Life was going on here in Coyacán at least five centuries before John Huss was burned at the stake.

The Aztec word "Coyoacán" means "The Place of Those

Who Have Coyotes." It was probably the market center for the red dogs which were sacrificed and buried with each person on his death. Unless accompanied by such a sacred red dog able to guide him and ferry him across the wide river on the way to Paradise, the dead man's soul would wander in eternal perdition. As I traversed the worn flaggings of the ancient town, plenty of mongrel descendants of the ancient breed snapped at my heels, advising me of my chance for personal salvation on my eventual journey.

Sometimes I walked to the beautiful Churubusco monastery, with its medieval embellished music texts in the choir loft behind the massive pipe organ. It contains a museum of Mexican-American war relics, tattered flags and bullet-smoked uniforms, mementoes of the brave cadets who were alleged to have leaped to their death from the ramparts of nearby Chapultepec rather than surrender. It is the Mexican Alamo.

Or I walked through winding flower-draped back lanes to San Angel to the handsome colonial inn. From its roofed terrace is a splendid view of the lordly snow volcanoes to the southeast, the Mountain of Smoke and the White Woman. I often ate there, de-luxe food to the music of marimbas or mariaches, under the patio arcades surrounding a plashing fountain and a garden luxurious with banana trees, oranges, scented floripondios, blood-red begonias, bougainvillaea, and lavender wisteria.

The season advanced. The luscious mangoes turned golden and finally disappeared from the fruit stands. Our garden had grown dilapidated, for José had gone off to the hot country without so much as an *adiós*. Petra grew irritated whenever I inquired about him. "He is away, señor," was all she would say, her lips tight.

One breathless warm night when I was sleeping in the raw, a mosquito—mosquitoes are infrequent at this altitude —bothered me, and I turned on the light to try to nail the pest. I was on my knees trying to find him when my head went around dizzily. The windows rattled violently, and the floor boards ground against each other as though being wrenched apart. An earthquake, and a bad one!

Snatching a blanket on the fly, I dashed to the middle of the patio. From there I could see a strange violet light jerking over the Pedregal lava. I know that seismologists claim that no visible electrical disturbance accompanies earthquakes, but my knowledge is too limited to provide any other explanation for the phenomenon I observed that night.

Coyotes howled, a spine-tingling wail, and dogs barked bitter answers far and near. In ran Petra and Lupe. "Are you all right, señor?"

I pulled my blanket a little closer. "It was *tremendo,* no!"

"For certain, the worst I have ever known, señor."

"Are Mario and María all right?"

"The *bichos* didn't even stop snoring."

"And you, Lupe, were you frightened?"

Her long lashes fluttered, and she pulled at the strap of her pink slip. "Very much, señor. I dropped on my knees to pray."

"And what did you pray for?"

"I couldn't pray, sinner that I am. I kept thinking, I want to scream, but I ought to pray, so I couldn't do either. Finally I told God, 'Father, this time I shall pray, but if you ever do this to us again, I'm going to scream.'"

II

WAFFLE WEDDING

IN the still of the night the moonlight ghosted along the pink wall. Behind the rear corral the great avenue trees rose up like a black mountain ridge. Out of the clear silence came a shrill piping.

Shortly after I rented the Coyoacán house a small, thin chap appeared in high boots and a shabby tan suit with leather buttons. Though it was hot noon, he had a woolen muffler wrapped tightly about his scrawny neck. He coughed hard. His big pistol and cartridge belt seemed too heavy for him.

His name was Gregorio. He explained that Coyoacán's

two policemen were unable to patrol all the dim streets properly, so many residents paid him to keep watch. Few serious crimes had ever been reported in this community, though four centuries ago Cortés was accused of having drowned his wife in a well. But—Gregorio drew his mouth down fearsomely—one could never tell.

"A green slip is fifty centavos a fortnight; a yellow slip, a peso," he explained.

"Please tell me about the green slips and yellow slips."

"For a green slip"—he coughed—"I pass by only twice each night. For a yellow slip, every hour."

"A yellow slip by all means," I said, though he looked scarcely able to tangle with a squirrel, let alone any real Tarzan situation.

He handed me a yellow slip, bearing a rubber stamp "Pagado" and his flourishing signature.

So it was that each hour of the night, as he raced along Ave María Street, he piped extra loud in front of my house. The night I woke to hear his piping was so hauntingly beautiful that I got up and stood at the patio door. The garden looked even more ragged, for José had not come back yet. Now, a big volunteer chayote vine was covering up bare spots and threatened to blanket the whole area. Its big leaves and large plump fruit glistened in the moonlight.

Petra did not like the chayote vine. Dourly she threatened "to cut its head off." I forbade this sternly. I marveled at the speed with which it transformed air, water, and soil into branches, leaves, and fruit. It climbed the side wall in a foam of green; greedily it mounted the back wall between patio and corral; it topped the charcoal shed with fierce curiosity; it flooded across the whole patio. Every day I had to lay a new long shoot aside to keep a path open. It was invading the house. A long branch pushed across the corridor steps near the front entrance. Now in the moonlight it quivered like a hundred living snakes. . . .

Petra, when she trotted home from market with her blue *rebozo* shawl draped over her head and her basket, muttered darkly at "the crazy vine." I teased her. "Where will the chayote go next?"

She flounced. "It will walk right into your room and strangle you in your sleep."

"Would you give me a nice funeral, Petra?"

A red jar she was carrying dropped and broke. "Señor, *por Dios!* It is nice to joke, but not about such things." She crossed herself.

On the night I stood watching in the moonlight, after I fell asleep again my dreams merged into a Gregorio in a Hindu turban piping to the chayote vine, which stood up like a score of cobras with raised hoods. Then a tropical rain came—I had been reading Bromfield's novel about India—and everything merged into deep liquid sleep.

When I woke again, sunlight was streaming in, and my servitors were already at their tasks. The day was gorgeous, the soft sun like a song; it was impossible to chain myself to my typewriter, and I burst out the front door and made the rounds of the market folk. It was Thursday—family day—so I dropped in at Pepe Calderón's house for lunch.

Pepe was a short, corpulent businessman with the heart of a poet—the sentimental moonbeam-and-roses variety. Lunch in his big colonial house near the plaza was a mighty institution, what with family, relatives, and friends. Today twenty-two of us sat at the big table under the gory game-fish paintings. Everybody was gabbing at once—a hilarious din in which no one could hear his or her neighbor and no-

body had any interest in doing so. Señorita Mercedes, a
niece, with flashing eyes and flashing jeweled fingers, told
juicy scandal about the mistresses of the minister of agriculture to General Cravioto, who was talking loudly, with nervous jabs at his small Hitleresque mustache, about the last
polo game. I looked around in amazement. Everybody was
engaged in a brilliant monologue, each entranced with the
sound of his voice. When anyone stopped for breath, he
would catch a phrase from the hashed din of words—"Fascism . . . the señorita at the ball . . . the high cost of living . . . bullfighting." What a din the last word created!
Each, having caught his own cue, rushed on with nervous
eagerness to expound his own ideas or experiences.

One smartly dressed girl, Marta Hoffman, not more than
eighteen, sat smiling silently with soft fruity lips and large
dreamy hazel eyes. Now and then her gold-globe earrings
quivered. She was holding her own inner monologue, and
from the warm flush on her cheeks it was a sweet one.

After lunch there was the usual prolonged session in the
big white stucco sala, with its shawl-draped grand piano
and stiff spindly chairs and settee. Don Pepe recited his
weekly poetic composition. His wife, buxom wheat-ripe Isabel, a former opera star, played the piano and sang her usual
bit, with encores, from the operas. Their little boy—this was
Pepe's second marriage—recited. He was intelligent and
likable, about seven, but dainty, with thin, sensitive features,
enormous eyes, and long lashes. Others were called upon to
contribute any notable talent. The rest of the afternoon was
spent in dancing.

My first duty was to dance with Leonor, the ninety-two-
year-old grandmother, who had presided at the head of the
table. It was a pleasant duty, for she was by all odds the

liveliest person in the room, lean and spry as a girl, with a
keen, bawdy mind. She was still undisputed head of the
matriarchal household, and no decision was ever made
without consulting her, be it the buying of a piece of furniture, or real estate or stocks. Her chief remembered glory
was that a famous Yucatán musician had written a song for
her when she was a girl, one of the popular hits of the day,
and the Thursday reunions always ended precisely at five
with Isabel at the piano and everybody present singing it.

My next dance partner, of course, was Isabel, incredibly
soft and stately. Then I asked Marta to dance. She lived
around the corner from me on the main avenue and, as
she often sat in the front window behind the iron *rejas,* we
already had scraped up a nodding acquaintance. She clung
to me with a deep sigh and seemed to grow more languid
and dreamy, then her nails dug sharply into my palm, and
she whispered fiercely, "I have to see you. May I come to
your house?"

From a Mexican girl of good family this was a startling
proposal, and I could feel the agitated rise and fall of her
breasts.

"Certainly. Or I will be glad to call on you."

"That won't do at all!" she whispered. "Mother must not
know about it. Nobody must know. Only you—and myself.
I have noticed that Petra and her tribe leave your house
every afternoon. Tomorrow, as soon as they are gone, I will
come over. Please leave your front door ajar so I can slip in
quickly unseen. I shall have to be on the lookout for that
gossipy girl who runs El Morenito and spends all her time
sitting in front."

True to her word, Marta slipped in breathlessly in a snug
light blue dress and blue turban. Her skin was so clear she

glistened. To hide the wild flurry of her feelings she talked about the patio flowers and the amazing chayote vine. Then the pounding rain came, almost drowning out our talk.

She perched on my couch, her shoulders drawn together, her palms pinched tightly between her knees. "You can't imagine how people gossip!" she began in a low, furious voice. "So you must realize what a risk I take in coming here this way."

Her gold bracelets clanked. "You can help me—if you will, but only if you truly wish to. It is an imposition, but I cannot confide in any Mexican friend."

Mexicans never relish coming to the point directly. After this prelude we talked aimlessly about Coyoacán, the Calderóns, the marvelous grandmother, and beautiful Isabel. Pepe's eldest son, by his first wife, was his spit image, short and corpulent and quite a ne'er-do-well, though he managed to hold good jobs. At present he had set up some dance-hall girl in an apartment as his mistress, and the agitated family was holding frequent reunions to discuss what best to do about the matter.

Marta got up nervously with a graceful lilt of her body and looked intently at the surrealist portrait an artist friend had made of me. All but one eye and a cheek were covered by a white horse.

"I don't think I understand it very well."

"The white horse probably symbolizes my literary genius, which is undoubtedly more important and attractive than my face."

Her story, when she finally told it, had to do with love and property. Despite popular romantic notions, they are nearly always intertangled. Her father—a Swiss married to a Mexican woman—had left his worldly possessions to be

divided equally among his widow and three children. Since
Marta was still under age, her share was still administered
by her mother. One of her brothers, a pharmacist, was trying
to get her mother to put everything into his hands. According to Marta he was a bad egg, a swaggering bully and
reckless spender, but able to twist his mother around his
finger. Already he had wheedled considerable sums out of
her.

Marta was secretly engaged to a boy who clerked for the
National Railways. Her mother had been nice to him until
she discovered he was poor. Marta now had to meet him
clandestinely. He, too, was under age, but Marta planned for
them to get married right away and sign a joint property
contract so he could lay immediate claim to her inheritance.
Would I be a witness at their marriage and tell a white lie
about their ages? Could I get some other friend, an American, to do the same?

She waited breathlessly, lovely as the dawn, and I could
not help feeling a twinge of disappointment that her secret
rendezvous with me was no sweet meat in my grinder.

"How can I help you, dear Marta?" I asked. "Neither your
marriage nor such a document will stand up in court. How
will that protect your property?"

"Oh, but it will. Once we are married, my share of the inheritance can be embargoed by the courts, and by the time
that is argued, we will be old enough to remarry if necessary.
Neither Mother nor my brother can touch it, not a cent."

"Suppose your mother has the marriage annulled right
off?"

"She'd never do that. As it is now, I can't protest or pre-
vent her putting everything into my brother's possession."
She clasped her hands beseechingly.

"Do you love this Antonio of yours very much?" I asked.

Her eyes turned to pure flame. "I'll never love anybody else. I'll wait a lifetime if I have to. I'll marry him if he doesn't have a tortilla. Naturally it will be easier if he can set up his own little business."

"You are sure Antonio loves you the same way?"

"He's more in love than I am, if that is possible."

"That's all that interests me. Your property is your own worry."

"Then you'll do it?" she cried, clasping her hands, her eyes brimming with happy tears.

"Antonio is a lucky dog. But before I promise, maybe I'd better meet the man of whom I am utterly jealous."

We arranged for him to come to my house the following afternoon. She would come separately, this time with a girl friend, so neighbors would not get suspicious and talk.

"Then in a few days I'll ask you to my house for tea so you can meet my mother. It will make things lots easier once she finds out that a nice, respectable person was our witness."

"That will be a new role for me. You'll have to provide the build-up. More likely when she hears the great news she'll think I'm a scoundrel and sick the dogs on me."

"Never! She's foolish and obstinate, but never unkind."

Marta's friend, Delia, was a flaming redhead, with milk-white skin and golden eyes, a petal mouth, and a hint of freckles across the bridge of her nose. She had a perfect hourglass figure, trim, nervous legs that seemed always impelled to dance. She pranced in with a gurgling laugh. Her gaiety had won her the nickname "Castanets." Marta was very pleased that I found her irresistible.

When Antonio showed up, we parked Delia in my study

while the three of us discussed the possible wedding plans.

Antonio was a fine, clean lad but without a third of Marta's ginger; she would be the manager of this combination. For all her dreaminess, she was superpractical. It was she who was making all the arrangements. But he worshiped her as a shining angel and, given his nature, always would. The match looked like a good bet. He was steady, polite, considerate, but in any real pinch Marta would keep the colors flying.

I left them alone presently and rejoined Delia, a pattern we continued to follow, for after that Marta and Antonio met each other in my place two or three times a week. Delia was all that I had ever hoped for. Don't tell me that good Samaritans are never rewarded.

Marta's tea party, though I was the only guest, was an event. Her house was stuffy with old, once costly furniture, a damp odor to everything. Her neurasthenic mother, not in good health, was difficult and arbitrary, although pathetically anxious to be nice. She was glad Marta had found a "proper friend" instead of "the inferiors" she was always taking up with.

"I have something special for you!" Marta told me proudly. She had bought an electric waffle iron merely to serve me an American delicacy. But the waffles came in stone cold, no butter, no syrup. I chewed and choked on leather, but said politely they were delicious.

On the day for signing the preliminary papers I picked Marta up in a taxi near the old Cortés palace. She wore a trim pearl-gray suit and tall patent-leather boots, and her face glowed with happiness and excitement. We collected Edda, an American newspaper girl, a broad blonde who loved fluffy dresses. Anxious to find out how Mexicans really live, she was thrilled to be in on a runaway marriage.

We went to the shabby registrar's office in the poor Pera-villo district. Antonio, because of a last-minute yard accident, arrived late, breathless and chagrined. The clerk said sourly that there was not enough time left to make out all the necessary documents.

Antonio accepted this verdict as unalterable and felt twice as mortified, but Marta flew right against the barricades. Her husband-to-be had to get special leave from work. Edda was an important, busy person; item, Mr. Beals. Antonio and I then joined in the chorus. The clerk kept arguing. The clock hands kept turning. But no Mexican will stop arguing as long as anybody wishes to argue. I am sure he would have kept on longer than it would have taken to prepare the papers. Not until I rattled some coins did a break come in the impasse.

"As a special concession to such charming people," he said, "we *might* work after hours." I rattled the silver coins louder, and he became almost eager to make such a concession.

"Nice business," Edda exploded in my ear. "Having to pay graft!"

"Take it easy. The little clerk's job is his only chance to feel important. That's true of bureaucrats the world over. How can they feel important unless they make obstacles for everybody? As for the extra pesos he will earn today by laboring honorably after hours, the poor devil makes only a pittance so they mean a lot to him. In how many lands in this world would a government bureau remain open two seconds after closing time? You get the window slammed shut in your nose."

The complicated papers were made out, certified health

certificates were presented, property contracts prepared for signing on the wedding day. All had to be copied laboriously in duplicate into two big black ledgers. We swore many times individually and collectively to many things.

Five days later we gathered in the court clerk's office in the ancient building that was entered from the Thieves' Market across from the National Palace. There was more delay, more rattling of coins in the pocket, but at last the numerous papers were all signed, sworn to, and copied into other big ledgers.

At long last, leaving a row of shiny coins on the desk of the court clerk, we filed into the dingy courtroom. A dusty Mexican flag was draped over the street window and a bust of Benito Juárez, Mexico's Lincoln. Rattly chairs lined the soiled cracked walls. The judge, enormously fat but meticulously attired in pin stripes, sat behind a splintered desk needing varnish, and mopped his putty face with a perfumed lavender handkerchief.

Wearily he stood up, scarcely deigning to notice us and, with a disdainful, bored air, shuffled the papers the obsequious clerk laid before him. His fleshy apricot lips moved as he read. Then he blew his nose, a mighty trumpeting that awesomely symbolized the majesty of the law. From behind Benito Juárez he took a silver monogrammed case and lit himself a cigarette and kept on reading, his cigarette dangling, his head tilted to keep the smoke out of his drowsy eyes. Suddenly, with a grandiloquent gesture, he shot back his not-too-clean cuffs and cleared his throat. Ancient stone tablets seemed to rattle on the mountaintops. "Hm," he grunted. "Everybody here? Everybody ready?"

Mechanically he mumbled over the marriage code and turned to Antonio. "Do you——"

A quick, slick individual in a check suit and maroon tie darted in. *"Ole, Licenciado!"* he sang out effusively. Antonio was left with his mouth hanging open.

The judge and his oily friend talked animatedly. They consulted lottery tickets and discussed the relative merits of the Michoacán and National lotteries. They passed little jokes and smirks about Linda Carmen, who apparently had all the necessary whatsit and amiability.

"Of all things!" sputtered Edda, her blue eyes blazing. But our Mexican friends, getting married, did not seem upset. If anything, they were enjoying the interruption.

The judge turned to his desk again, shuffled his papers, cleared his throat, creased his eyes pompously, and restored the full majesty of the law. Once more he began in his fat purple voice. But just as Antonio's mouth was open to say, "I do," Check Suit darted in again to whisper slyly about a case of cognac for the party, then vanished with a knowing leer.

The plump judge passed his lavender handkerchief over his smooth olive jowls, adjusted his cuffs, and once more proceeded with the sacred ceremony. Just as Antonio's mouth was open a third time to say "I do," the clerk, frantically waving, caught the judge's eye. The latter was reminded that he had neglected to interrogate the witnesses.

We nodded affirmatively, with our hands lifted, to queries about our ages, nationality, residence, marital status, height, color of our hair and eyes, and what more I don't recall. The judge gave Edda quite an eye. She choked with fury.

Again he mumbled the blessed words over Antonio. "Do you? . . ."

"I do!" roared Antonio with such energy and volume it shook the dust loose, almost as if he were afraid he would never get another chance to say it. The judge looked hurt.

Marta had to swear to a special obedience clause. "Do you? . . ."

"I do."

"You are married," thundered the judge with a regal glare but with a certain triumph.

His bored look vanished. He beamed cat fashion. He bowed low and chivalrously over Marta's hand. He held Edda's hand with a deep-sea sigh. Edda was thirtyish, neat, but full of figure and—*blond*. The judge smirked coyly. But it was I to whom the judge paid special attention, for from me would come the fee. He pumped my hand mightily and followed it up with friendly pats. I slipped him the customary gold piece. He winked, tilting his head in Edda's direction, with a rolling motion of his hands shaping her configuration. "How you say it in the English, she is very speefy."

He shoved the coin into his white vest pocket, and the froglike mask fell over his face again. He turned away with a little wave of dismissal.

Belatedly I kissed Marta. "I guess it wasn't a young girl's dream of a fine marriage, but . . ."

She squeezed my arm, her eyes brimming with happiness. "It was a gorgeous wedding, and it was you who made it possible. I'd kiss you a hundred times if it wouldn't make Antonio jealous."

"For goodness' sake let him be jealous."

She laughed and stroked the gardenias he had brought her.

I took them to an upstairs restaurant at an outside balcony table on Sixteenth of September Street. "Let us," I suggested, "order waffles."

Marta watched me butter mine and pour on syrup.

Then she tried hers. "Why, these are good!" She laughed and laughed. "I thought you Americans had awfully queer tastes in food. And when I served you those terrible cold waffles, you sat there chewing and choking like I did, never saying an impolite word. And they say you Americans are tactless! No Mexican would have stood for it."

I had arranged to stay over night in the city so the couple could have my house, the only honeymoon they would get. Marta had convinced her mother she was going, properly chaperoned, to a party which would probably last most of the night.

When I returned the next day, Gregorio was watching at my door with a long face. "Señor, it is serious or I would not have gone without my needed sleep today, waiting here to see you. Last night," he began with a cough, "a dreadful thing happened."

"Tell me!" I clutched his arm.

"A strange man was trying to pick your lock. As I rounded the corner he fled. But when I made my rounds again later, he had your door open. I chased him inside. He drew a gun on me."

"Go on."

"Fortunately he tripped on your chayote vine, or I would now be serenading only St. Peter with my whistle. That vine is all that saved my life, your chayote vine, señor. I pounced on him then, señor. No cat could have gotten a rat more neatly. I am not so large, señor, but I know well the *hui hitso* [jujitsu]. I planted my knee on his back and twisted his arm. He had a chicken heart. He screamed for mercy. I led him off to the police station meek as a lamb. He is there now, being held till you prefer charges."

"What did he tell you?"

"The shameless animal claimed his sister was inside with you, and he was going to kill you." Gregorio shook his head lugubriously. "A most violent, headstrong man, señor. I told him you were wholly respectable, a caballero who would never sleep with a girl unless it were her ardent wish, that for him to break into your house was a crime punishable by law. Besides that, I know now you were not even home."

"Did you see anyone come out?"

He twisted one of his leather buttons. "Señor, I am an honorable nightwatchman. I saw nothing. For a second it seemed as though I saw two figures, but the starlight must have played tricks on my eyesight. There was a rustle of leaves over yon wall . . ."

"You are an honor to your profession, Gregorio. The poets also see stars that are so bright they see nothing else."

"That, too, is my profession, señor." He started to draw out a manuscript.

"We'd better get right down to the police station," I said hurriedly, and slipped him several pesos for his trouble.

Police headquarters were in the old red-stone Cortés Palace on the plaza. I walked a nice tightrope, convincing the police that Gregorio had done his duty well and nobly, that it was all my fault, I had neglected to tell him that Marta's brother was coming to see me at a late hour. An unfortunate misunderstanding. He was crestfallen, apologetic, really charming, but I could tell Marta was wholly justified in not wanting him to get hold of her money.

When I got back to the house, just before the heavy afternoon thunderstorm, I stood at the doors, watching the big white drops crash on the chayote leaves with almost metallic reverberation. Had it not been for that preposterous exuberant vine there might have been a tragedy. It was better than a watchdog. An octopus could have done no better.

Petra hurried in from the storm with her blue *rebozo* and basket. Near the front entrance she looked at the chayote branch across the steps and muttered darkly. Pouring though it was, she determinedly plunked down her laden basket and smacked a big stone on top of the shoot near the edge of the steps. "You have gone far enough!" she scolded.

Then she saw me standing in the doorway. A sheepish grin spread over her worn walnut face, and she trotted on to the kitchen.

III

LUPE'S BIRTHDAY CAKE

IT was still too early for my neighbor's "Anchors Aweigh." What brought me bolt upright in bed was the agonizing hee-haw of a burro. His long ears poked through the laced brick parapet, and he was grinning insolently into my bedroom.

Petra swished by. María came pattering. I heard Lupe sing out. Mario's long-handled twig broom was leaning un-used against the balustrade. Something unusual had erupted in my establishment.

Not one burro but six were knee-deep in the chayote vine and wrenching at it with greedy teeth. The entrance tiles now needed a scrubbing, not just a sweeping. The center of

this commotion was a gigantic Indian well over six feet. He
looked like a Hollywood buccaneer, overalls tucked in his
high boots and a wicked knife hilt protruding from his wide
crimson sash. Bound around his head, under his enormous
straw sombrero, was a red bandanna. All he lacked were
gold earrings. His face was black with charcoal dust, and he
was dumping six loads of charcoal into the adobe shed.

Petra came running, her seamed face worried. "I pray,
señor, that you approve that I have bought all this charcoal.
It is a real bargain, much less than what I pay in the market
by the basketful."

"I've told you many times to get in a supply."

"Gabriel"—she indicated the big pirate—"smuggles it
across the Pedregal so he pays no taxes, which are much."

"Do you think we ought to cheat the government, Petra?"

She drew a line on the tiles with her worn brown shoe.
"That is always a good thing, señor, if you can do it, and this
is the finest grade charcoal, mostly oak, and fifty centavos
less a load . . . Señor . . ." She clasped her hands beseechingly.

From then on we bought all our charcoal from Gabriel.
He and his animals did not exactly trumpet into our heavenly patio, they came surging in with bellows and brays and
voracious lunges at everything edible.

Gabriel paid no attention to pretty, flirtatious Lupe, but
he rolled fierce eyes at little chicken-legged María, with a
cascade of fine talk. It put her in a great flutter.

This was another gorgeous morning, and after breakfast
I burst out the door, debating whether to clamber across
the Pedregal or go to the plaza. Rosalinda, the buxom girl
who ran El Morenito, was sitting in front rolling her ample
bosom to greet the joyous early sun. All she sold were cheap

cigarettes, scratch pads, penny pencils, cones of brown piloncillo sugar, salt, flyspecked tins of sardines, and withered fruit, so how she made a living was hard to conjecture, but she was always singing or laughing or chattering to neighbors the livelong day. Mostly she basked in the sun at her door, her large black eyes alert for every movement in the narrow street.

"*Buenos días,* Rosalinda. What a beautiful day!"

"*Buenos días,* Don Carletón. We are truly blessed."

"Do you know Don Gabriel, the charcoal man?"

"That devil! Someday he will hang by the heels, mark my words. Did he have his little burro pray for you?"

"That is something I must see. The next time he comes."

She put her hands together and lifted her large breasts in agonized piety. "The little burro sits up with his hoofs together like this and brays his prayers."

"Tell me, Rosalinda, are there ghosts and hobgoblins in the Pedregal?"

She looked at me big-eyed. "I never believed you *gente de razón* put stock in such things. There must be dreadful ones. Where could unhappy souls be happier than in such a wild, lonely, topsy-turvy place? This I do know. Some years ago a terrible bandit lived in the very middle of the lava flow in a straw hut so well concealed that the police could never flush him out. He robbed houses on the edge and killed many people and scattered their heads far and wide. *Dios,* what a terrible monster!"

"Aren't you afraid, living alone here so close by?"

"Ho! What have I to be afraid of? The poor are never bothered, and I'm not so pretty that I have to fear what some girls do."

"You're plenty pretty, Rosalinda. If I were a bandit, I'd

make a beeline to your place. You are nice and brown and soft—like the name of your little store—with sunlight and sweetness in you."

Archly she asked, "Why don't you have a girl, a real pretty one, till someday you wish to get married?"

"Only one?"

"For shame!" She gurgled. "Señor, are you one of those who must have a different pair of arms each night?"

She rose to wait on a customer. Rolling her hip at me, she winked. "Perhaps I'll come over and see that you behave yourself."

I walked along winding Benito Juárez Avenue where the sidewalks are tilted up in cement cakes by the roots of big trees. Don Nacho, a strip of twisted dried leather that had taken on the shape of an old man, sat against a house wall, his long, bony legs across the pavement. His polished yellow cane, with a carved coyote head, and his tall peaked sombrero lay beside him. I dropped the usual five centavos into the brim. "How's business, Don Nacho?"

"As God wills it, so it is always good, today and always." He smiled shyly. "And today God wills I have little rheumatism. I feel like a young man."

"Don't tell me," I said sternly, "that you sit this way on the sidewalk so as to eye the pretty girls' ankles."

He chuckled. "They do look prettier on days when my rheumatism doesn't talk back." He paused. "Someday, señor, I may tell you about *her*."

As I climbed and jumped across the rocky Pedregal I thought of Lupe. Lately she'd had such a reckless gleam in her eye that I feared she might fly the coop again. I'd have to do something. Nothing is dearer to a Mexican's soul than a fiesta, and Lupe's saint's day was coming up. When

I got home I told Petra to buy a turkey, make *mole* sauce, and we'd celebrate the occasion.

Petra's face glowed. "You are too kind, señor! I will make a nice fiesta for Lupe and all of us. The turkeys come to market very lean. It will be cheaper to buy one now and fatten him up. . . ." *Guajolote* was the word she used for "turkey," which in Aztec means "Rattle Bird."

She came back with a huge skinny fowl. His long gray wattles were different from those of a New England turkey, but there are many more varieties in Mexico, which was the original home of the turkey. This specimen gobbled angrily and fled to hide his head ostrich fashion in the farthest corner of the corral. Not even scattered corn enticed him forth. But in a few days he brightened up and came running to eat corn out of my hand. Soon he followed Petra or me around like a puppy. When I took my morning splash, he would stand alongside gobbling. After a few weeks the friendly soul got into the habit of coming to my door at daybreak and gobbling until I woke up and cursed him. This cheekiness was too much, so I shut him up securely in the back corral.

Several days before the fiesta Petra sharpened the butcher knife and ordered María to kill him.

María came back blubbering that she had grown too fond of him.

"You big crybaby," scoffed Lupe. She lifted one knee, pulling her stocking tighter under her red garters, and seized the butcher knife. But she, too, came back crestfallen.

"What's a girl going to do?" she asked with a fillip of her shoulder. "He looked at me with his red eyes and talked friendly way down in his throat. He would haunt me if I killed him."

Petra gave a disgusted snort. Grumbling mightily, she headed for the shed with resolute stride, knife in hand. Soon she came back and beelined to me.

"None of us can kill him, señor. It's a woman's job, but perhaps this once . . ." She held forth the butcher knife.

I eyed it dubiously. "In my country, Petra, it is wicked to kill a bird by slitting its throat. A hatchet makes it all right, but we have no hatchet."

"I understand, señor. You do many things differently."

There was a terrific pounding at the front portal. María flew to investigate.

In surged Gabriel's burros with the balance of our charcoal order. They dashed eagerly to the chayote vine, teeth flashing greedily. Gabriel followed with a wide swagger, plucking his stringy mustache, white teeth sparkling in his begrimed face, and making eyes at María. When he found that even the master of the house was afraid to kill a turkey, he laughed with gleeful superiority and tested the edge of Petra's blade with his thumb. Presently he emerged from the shed proudly, wiping the blood off on his trousers.

I asked about his praying burro.

"Little Don Diego!" He whistled, and the smallest animal came over, sat down, clapped his forehoofs, then sank his head and brayed, an anguished prayer.

Gabriel knotted the money I paid him in the end of his crimson sash. "And the turkey, señor? Killing the turkey with such a brave heart, is that not worth a tequilita, a little drink? There are no taverns on the long miles across the Pedregal."

He eyed my tip thoughtfully. "And little Diego, my burrito, for his nice tricks, should he not have a fresh carrot or lump of sweet piloncillo?"

I gave him another tip. As he left, he leaned down and lifted a caterpillar with a leaf from the gravel path and put it among the vines. "The poor little fellow might get stepped on," he said, this fierce pirate with bloodstained pants.

Petra spent two days cooking the turkey, grinding spices, combining herbs and turkey sauce. Every little while something would be missing, and María or Mario would fly to the plaza grocery.

Lupe's saint's day was that of the great national religious festival, Guadalupe Day, celebrated every December 12, in a suburb north of the capital. I invited Edda and several visiting American friends to take in the celebration and sample Petra's *mole* afterward. We planned to get out for the colorful predawn Mass, so I borrowed Edda's alarm clock to be sure to get up on time.

It was pitch dark when I shivered along Ave María Street, and I had to walk to the plaza before I found a taxi. It is customary for the chauffeur and hirer to compare their timepieces so as to avoid later arguments. The chauffeur had no watch. When I thrust the luminous hands of Edda's clock at him, he almost jumped out of the car. He crossed himself energetically.

"It is a strange watch, señor, a big one to be carrying around, and why does it have devil hands? I hope it plays no nasty tricks on me."

Already, before dawn, the road out of the city was jammed with traffic and lined with foot pilgrims, cripples, the maimed, the halt, and the blind, hoping to be cured this sacred day by the waters of the Holy Well. Even elegantly dressed women were going on their knees in the dust the whole five miles.

The Mass was dense with incense and flowers and the

acrid body odor of thousands of pack-jammed Indians and
peasants. We wandered past the carnival booths, merry-go-
rounds, and Ferris wheel, the eating places and the stalls of
rosaries and relics and beautifully wrought candles. We
bought dyed straw necklaces, beads and sashes and pottery
and good-luck "deer eyes," big, polished seeds supposed to
have miraculous powers. We munched on sweet tiny corn-
cakes colored venomous greens and blues and reds, just as
the Aztecs had in religious festivals here hundreds of years
before the Spaniards came.

The winding adobe-walled lane to the summit of Tepeyac
hill was lined with photographers supplied with wondrous
scenery. Travelers from remote corners of Mexico wish some
such memento to show less-fortunate neighbors. For most
folk this pilgrimage is the highlight of a lifetime.

Edda and I picked the particular backdrop we desired. I
straddled a wooden burro before a painting of the holy
shrine with an airplane circling overhead. Edda stuck her
blond head through a hole in the canvas, which made her
seem to be leaning out of the plane over the golden towers
and maguey fields. Hovering over us, treading a billowy
painted cloud, blessed Virgin Guadalupe, clad in a star-
studded blue robe, clasped her tiny hands in adoration.

The church and cemetery atop Tepeyac hill were also
crowded with pilgrims and vendors of candles and holy
tracts. A ragged Indian on a stepladder was busily scrubbing
a white marble angel over a tomb to limpid purity with soap-
suds and zacate fiber, although his own grimy face probably
had never known soap. Below us stretched the sun-drenched
Anahuac Valley and the golden towers of Mexico City,
ringed by lofty purple volcanoes, this day touched with
snow.

Every pilgrim visits the Holy Well to drink the miraculous waters, sprinkle them over wrists and face, and take home a bottle for future use. The sick and ulcerating are most anxious to secure this blessing, and as we edged forward body to body an inch at a time, we were probably in contact with as great a single assortment of varied and concentrated germs and viruses as was to be found in any space of the same size anywhere on the face of the globe.

Someone gave me a wallop on the back of the head. I looked around angrily but met only brown-faced stares. When we returned to Coyoacán and I put my hand into my overcoat pocket to show the taxi driver the hour, the alarm clock was gone, and I knew the meaning, then, of the jolt on my skull at the Holy Well.

"I'm not surprised," the chauffeur told me. "It must have returned to the lower regions from which it originally came."

"I only hope its luminous hands scare the thief."

"Unhappy man! A clock that spits light, he will believe the devil is after him because of his evil deed."

Since proof of the exact time had vanished, the chauffeur charged me for an extra hour.

"I shall not argue," I told him. "But remember, the devil pursues the evil of heart."

He crossed himself. "Clearly it is God's will that you lost the big watch. It is also God's will that I remember the time so exactly. Besides, two pesos are two pesos."

Petra's fine *mole* and fixings, black beans and rice, were a grand success. After my guests had gone, that evening it became wholly Lupe's celebration. She had invited a girl friend and an old aunt. Petra had on her one good dress of brown satin. María was almost pretty in a nice print dress; her hair, which she had been caring for better since the arrival of Gabriel, was rolled up shiny. Lupe wore gold-green rayon, tight as glass on her slim curves, and fiery earrings which I had bought her as today's birthday present.

I put on a record and made Petra dance. After a few clumsy turns she clucked like a hen and fled giggling to the kitchen. But Lupe pressed her body to me and rotated her hips in the *danzón* ecstatically.

I had bought a big cake with candles, explaining it was a birthday custom in my country where we always did things "different." The stars in Lupe's eyes matched the flickering candles. I told her to blow them out in one breath, those left burning would indicate the years till she got married.

She got to laughing and blew out only three. Ruefully she counted the fourteen that remained. "Why, I'll be an old lady by then!"

A few weeks later Petra was going around with a long face. Lupe had run off with another chauffeur. "He's another no-account," she fumed. "I warned her she will regret it."

In another two weeks Lupe was back, weeping and repentant.

"It's good to have Lupe back," I told Petra.

She was relieved that I took it quite naturally. "*Como no,* señor! It's nice. The little fool! Just as I warned her!"

"Did you scold her properly?"

"Only a little, señor. Since she's not going to marry for fourteen years, how could you expect her to do anything else? Plainly it was God's will."

"Lupe's prettiness as well as God and the candles, I suspect, had considerable to do with it."

"It was God's will," repeated Petra firmly. "But there may be a silver lining—if God also wills we have another mouth to feed. In time there will also be another worker."

IV

CANTINA BRAWL

SOMEONE was shaking me, and I came up from the mat of sleep fighting.

"It's time to get up!" Petra stood by my bed with a small ocote torch shining through her transparent yellow fingers. "The electric lights are off." She sniffed disgustedly. Her face was an oval of illuminated gold in her closely drawn *rebozo*.

A party of us was going to climb Mount Ajusco, the fourteen-thousand-foot cone south of Mexico City, and we had to catch an early train. It was a chill morning, and I washed my face Jeeters' style, three flicked drops and a shudder. I was still shivering as I pulled on my boots. My cap, purchased in Vera Cruz, was an elegant salt-and-pepper job with button straps of which I was quite fond.

The train climbed out of the valley in screeching figure eights above the age-old brown towers, the silver sheen of lakes, and the bower of willow and ash trees around the Xochimilco floating gardens. We could see the series of runty volcanic cones strewn across the east side of the valley floor and beyond, sixty miles distant, the soaring snow crests of the volcanoes.

The air, when we descended at high Ajusco station, was still thin and cold, and we stepped briskly along toward the village of thatched huts and bell towers several miles along the ridge. We would have to hustle to beat the midday heat to the crest, then make it back in time to catch the night train. The altitude soon pounded in our chests. My friend Ernest, a portly editor just down from the States, was not in condition for this fast pace. Beyond the village he could not keep up, and I lagged behind with him. The others were soon out of sight. About a fourth of the way to the top we took the wrong trail. It grew dimmer and finally petered out.

This was discouraging, for it was a long way back down the mountain to the fork. As the woods here were fairly open, with little underbrush, we hoped that by stiff climbing we could regain the main trail. But the way got rougher with fallen trees and big boulders till it became dangerous. The ascent was getting steeper, and a great cliff yawned below us. The sun was out hot now, perspiration bathed us, though when we sat down, which we had to do ever more frequently, the breeze was chilly. We may have reached two thirds to the summit when Ernest was hit by *soroche,* or mountain sickness, a more terrifying and unpleasant affliction than seasickness. It puts a great strain on the heart, and it was a long time before he felt well enough to stir again.

There was nothing to do but return by slow stages. It was pitch dark when we reached the village. The place had no electricity, and the only lights were the faint gleams of charcoal fires and ocote torches through the wattled walls. At a hut on the outskirts I asked how to get to the station. A lean Indian in white pajamas courteously left his straw mat where he was chewing supper before a red brazier and told us which way to go.

But we lost our way. One by one the lights in the huts were going out; soon the village lay in murky darkness. We lost all trace of the footpath and bumped into barbed wire and cactus fences. We drove off barking curs. Maguey thorns tore at us. How many acres of corn we trampled down I have no idea. We fell into a brook.

"We've missed the train by now!" wailed Ernest. "Whatever will we do? We'll die in a place like this." He was genuinely frightened.

I assured him any Indian would gladly put us up for the night in his hut. I had often lived for months in primitive Indian villages, sleeping on straw mats, eating native tortillas and chile, so the situation did not strike me as dour. But Ernest, who had a doctor's degree, was making a detailed study of Mexican diseases and sanitation, or lack of it. He pictured himself coming down with typhoid, typhus, smallpox, yaws, malaria, leprosy, elephantiasis, enteritis—everything. This fear put new energy into him. He began breathing heavily. Alarmed, I took his arm. Suddenly he vanished from my side. The future governor of a great American commonwealth disappeared—in a most undignified fashion. He had fallen into a deep pit. He was blubbering with anger and fright when I pulled him out.

After about an hour we hit a broad trail again—at the hut where I had first made inquiries. We had made a huge circle. The hut was now dark. I called several times, and the tall Indian finally woke up. We explained our plight and, while we stood shivering in our wet clothes, for an icy wind was blowing off the mountain, patiently and courteously he gave us directions again. Ernest insisted I ask him to accompany us. Though not anxious to face that cutting night air, the Indian rigged up an ocote torch shielded by brown paper, pulled a sarape about his bony shoulders, and led the way down a rocky gulch.

"Has the train gone yet?"

"That I would not know, señores."

Ernest thought the station would be the best place to spend the night, but with our wet clothes and no food or blankets, it was the poorest bet of all. I asked our guide if we could sleep at his place.

"Certainly, señor. But we are poor, not even an extra petate or sarape. I can find you a better place."

We moved on silently. The Indian's loose white trousers flapped about his bony ankles. His one-thong sandals slapped the stones. Courteously he warned us of bad ruts and pitfalls. Finally on our left we saw the station lights. It meant the train had not come yet.

We found the others already there, though they had gone to the top. Ernest was so grateful to our guide that he emptied out his pockets, a double handful of coins which was probably more than the Indian would ever see in a month of toil.

The train, had it been on time and we had made it, would have gotten us back to Mexico City in time for a late dinner. We had to content ourselves with an apple and a bar of chocolate. By the time the train arrived, more than two hours late, we were frozen through. The ride itself was a torture, for the train seemed determined to be as late as possible. All the way we got colder, and by the time we got to Buena Vista Station in the city, nearly midnight, our teeth were chattering.

I suggested we stop in a dance cantina across the street and get a hot rum punch, but Ernest was too keen on getting home and taking a bath in the hope of staving off the dread diseases he was sure he might get. I went to the cantina by myself.

It was a typical place with a bar, tiled dance floor, rear and side booths filled with drinkers, and gaudily clad hostesses. I sidled up to the end of the bar and asked for a hot rum punch, drawing my cap low and paying no attention to anybody.

A fluffy creature in yellow, short below and short above, shoved her softness against my shoulder. "Dance with me."

"Not tonight, Pretty One."

She leaned closer. "Buy me a drink then."

"Not tonight, my dear."

"All right. Just give me a hug and a kiss and I'll go." She moved her hip against me and put up her mouth.

When I declined her offering, she put her hands on her hips and said, with blazing eyes, "At least give me a cigarette!"

She stuck it behind her ear near the red flower in her black hair and went off, shaking herself gaily, with a flash of golden garters and skin.

I sipped the hot punch gratefully and thawed out. I was feeling like a human being again, when a hearty American voice sounded at my elbow. "Hey, boy, have a drink on me."

My bones ached, I was in no mood for some American slummer or down-and-outer. The Negro lad who grinned at me was handsome and well built. I pointed to my hiking clothes and told him I was dead tired. "But I'll buy you a drink."

"Make it ginger ale," he replied to my surprise. "I'm a prizefighter."

He showed me a green handbill with his smiling features looking over a raised glove. He had just fought the Mexican welterweight champ in the bull ring and had won and was now blowing off steam.

He insisted I meet his girl. "It won't take but a minute," he said, over my protests that I wasn't dressed and was tired. "She's sweet and pretty. Boy, is she sweet!" He deposited me in a rear booth and came back with one of the hostesses clad in a scandalous sheer red dress.

Rosa was a cute trick, with curly black hair, enormous black eyes, lots of sparkle. She really liked the prizefighter, whom she called "Juan," or "Johnny" with a charming accent.

For himself he ordered a Tehuacán fizz water; for Rosa green *menta,* probably colored water at a fancy-drink price; for me, another hot rum punch. We toasted to our various healths. Paying Rosa the usual compliments, I prepared a quick getaway. "Some other night, when I'm dressed right, I'll spend a gay night with you and Johnny."

I had laid my cherished salt-and-pepper cap on the edge of the table. Rosa tried it on at a rakish angle and eyed her appearance in a hand mirror with satisfaction.

Out on the tiled floor couples were whirling about. Up on a green platform suspended from the ceiling an orchestra was energetically sawing and blowing and thumping a stirring *danzón*. A burly customer at the bar, half-seas over, was growing boisterous. Underneath his watermelon paunch he wore a double-laced cartridge belt and a .48. Sticking out his foot, he tripped up a waitress. By luck and ingenuity she saved her tray of bottles and glasses. Putting it down on the bar, she let fly a syphon in his face.

Wiping his dripping jowls with his sleeves, he snatched up another syphon bottle and took after her.

She dashed screaming straight toward our booth. Yanking the door shut on its overhead rollers, she dived in, landing on my lap. She was no featherweight, round above as round below, broad in the beam in every latitude.

Too tipsy to figure out how the sliding door worked, the burly drunk tried to yank it open. Finally he lifted one side and let fly with his syphon. The sharp stream hit Johnny's knee.

"*Cabrón!* You big goat!" he yelled. This is an ugly fighting word, and the drunk outside whipped out his gun. Letting out a roar, he kicked and battered at the door.

With one slash of his arm Johnny swept our glasses from the table and yanked a gun out of an armpit holster. Here I was in a corner, trying to extricate myself from the twitching tallow on my lap.

Rosa threw herself on Johnny. "Don't shoot, Juan! Please don't shoot!"

"Want the idiot to kill me?" he shouted, tossing her aside.

She was up and at him like a flashing tigress. The man outside kept lunging like a mad bull, and Johnny tried to free himself from Rosa, but she clung to him fiercely.

"Rosa, you little fool!" he cursed softly. "Get out of the way! Get down on the floor quick!"

"Juan, give me your gun. For God's sake don't shoot! I

love you, Juan! You mustn't do it! You can't! You mustn't!"

The door shivered violently. There might be some safety in this narrow cubbyhole by crawling ignominiously under the table. That is where I had dumped Lump of Tallow. Whimpering with terror, like a whipped puppy, she pulled her silk dress up over her head as if to shut out the menace. The way Johnny's pistol was gyrating in his struggle with Rosa, the waitress's plump bare posterior promised to be the first target.

The rhinoceros outside hurled his two hundred pounds plus against the flimsy door and lunged through like a full-back hitting the line. The door splintered from its roller and pivoted in the middle.

I was already standing on the seat, and I dived across the table through the opposite half of the door and took the tiled dance floor on my shoulder and slid.

A shot rang out. Then another.

As I clawed the polished tiles, I saw legs and whirling silk dresses flying to the street—a crazy whirl of hashed-up color and motion. Half-a-dozen hostesses huddled in the safest corner, like an animated heap of confetti, yelping or screaming. But several blasé girls sat in the booths calmly sipping their drinks and chattering as if nothing unusual were happening. Up front, the yellow-dress girl was crouching behind the corner, seizing the opportunity to eat a rolled taco. "Have one," she said gaily. "It's safe enough here."

Two waiters vaulted the bar on the dead run toward the booth. The police would be in any second. Not anxious to get mixed up in any such mess, I hit the sidewalk in three more jumps.

The air was cool on my flushed face, and I rubbed my bruised side and numbed arm. Rosa still had my cap on her bonny head. There was no reason to go off without it. I poked my nose through the swinging doors. One of the waiters waved me back with his apron. Human upheaval continued around the booth. Then I saw the big ox go down. He lay stiff on the tiles, not moving. But I could see neither Johnny nor Rosa.

Up on the green platform the musicians were cautiously poking tousled heads from behind the big drum. Back of the bar, Yellow Fluff was still planted on her gilded haunches with a show of golden garters, washing her taco down with long swigs from a bottle. Two gendarmes came tearing down the street, blowing their whistles, and I jumped away from the door. They pounded on inside.

I was about to have another look when Rosa came tearing out. She still wore my cap. Behind her, knees pumping hard, raced one of the policeman. Drawing his gun, he ordered her to halt. Lifting her skirts high, she flew on down the block, past the drawn iron shutters, the law hard after her. I flew after them both.

She darted into a cheap station hotel at the corner. The policeman followed close behind. I skidded in, right on their heels.

"Give me the gun," he ordered.

It became a clawing, scratching match, no holds barred. Her hair fell over one blazing eye. Her thin scarlet dress was ripped from shoulder to waist, and her bare breasts heaved from the struggle and her fury. She drew a bloody gouge down his cheek.

I danced around on the outskirts of the fray, trying to reach over and snatch the cap from her head. Her necklace broke, and the stones rolled across the floor. The tatters of her bright dress rippled like fire and fluttered like the colors jabbed into the shoulder of the prize bull in the ring.

The gendarme got a partial grip on the gun she had hidden under her skirt and twisted, but she hung on grimly, biting and kicking. The flashing barrel pointed every which way, and the hotel employees ducked out. Trying to keep out of range of that fast-moving weapon, I still tried to get hold of my cap.

Why did I take such risk of being shot by that crazy gun, even though fond of that piece of apparel, I do not know. Maybe it was a trick of my brain, a subconscious desire to be part of the wild melodrama, maybe the rum punches were talking. Just as I snatched the headgear off her curls, the gun went off with a roar.

I felt of myself. "Brother," I told myself, "it's high time you hotfooted it home to bed." But curiosity rooted me to the spot.

Why had Rosa run off with Johnny's gun? Had he been carrying it without a permit? Had he shot the big drunk and was she trying to cover up? Was Johnny all right? Or had he also been shot?

I was fired by an impulse to go back and see. At the same time I wanted to see what happened to Rosa. Common sense told me to go on home. I could not be in three places at once.

Rosa stood there, sucking her breath in and out in angry gasps, her exposed torso rising and falling. She was sobbing furiously over the loss of the gun.

The policeman tamped the bloody gouges in his cheek and pulled out a little black book. She snapped insolent replies while trying to tie the shreds of her dress together to hide herself a bit. Losing patience with her snap-turtle answers, he grabbed her roughly to lead her off.

Again she fought him, biting, clawing, kicking, step by step, jerk by jerk across the lobby. He got more mean shin bruises, another gouge, and her repairs to her dress were undone.

Johnny dashed in, a lean streak of lightning. "Let her go!" he ordered the policeman.

"The louse got your gun away from me," Rosa exclaimed, still struggling.

Juan advanced menacingly. "Hand it over, you *Cabrón!*" he shouted.

The policeman let go of Rosa. His hand shot to the gun at his belt.

Johnny swung fast. He packed dynamite. Never have I seen any man go down so fast, so like a lump of senseless lead. Juan grabbed Rosa in his arms and kissed her.

The gendarme writhed and groaned, rolled over twitching, finally got to his hands and knees, his mouth slobbering. Groggy, shaking his ears, he stared dizzily at Johnny's legs. After a few more groans he stood up, swaying unsteadily. Johnny yanked out a card and thrust it under his nose. It was a Mexico secret-service card. He outranked the policeman.

Those days it was customary to give such cards to visiting sports celebrities. Or maybe Johnny's prizefighting was a blind. Apparently not even Rosa had known this about her sweetheart. She gasped, wide-eyed.

Johnny lifted his gun off the policeman, broke it, whirled the chamber, squinting to see how many bullets were left. Snatching the officer's little black book, he tore it to shreds. "Now scram! *Sacate! Sacate!*" he said, using a word ordinarily only for animals. "Scram fast unless you want more of the same."

The policeman scurried out like a scared rabbit. Johnny drew Rosa into the circle of his arm, yanked a key off the rack, hook and all, and swept her upstairs. I watched her tattered fluttering dress, her bare back and side, the convulsive movement of her trim legs as Johnny rushed her along so fast her high-heeled red shoes scarcely touched every third step. She was certainly a neat trick, and I felt a twinge of envy at the passionate climax Juan had provided to the evening's show.

Curiosity took me back to the cantina. It was blaring as though nothing had happened. The orchestra was sawing and tooting with more than usual jungle-tune flourish. Couples were hugging, kissing, rotating their hips in the *danzón*. Garish laughter rang out. Lump of Tallow was toting bottles with a busy rush. She flashed me a comradely smile.

There in plain view in the nearest booth was the big ox who had started the rumpus. His head was on his arms, and he was sobbing as though his heart would break. Yellow Fluff, the girl who had first accosted me, had one arm about his neck and was petting him consolingly.

"So they didn't lock him up," I said to the bartender.

"Naw! Nobody got hurt, except the black boy laid the big fellow out with one wallop, colder than a dog's nose."

"But the *cuicos*, the cops?"

"A couple of pesos to them fixed everything up. But they lifted the big boy's gun because he had no license. That's what he's bawling about now."

The damp in my clothes settled in my bones again. I shivered and, thinking of Johnny and Rosa snug in each other's arms, I felt lonely. Yellow Fluff was beelining toward me again. I got out fast.

As my taxi turned into dimly lit Ave María over the mossy cobbles, Gregorio came running along, piping his "Three o'clock and all's well!"

I showed him my cap. He turned it over in his hands. "It's a nice cap," he conceded.

"I'll say it is," I answered, and went inside and hit the hay.

I dreamed that Ernest and I were trapped in a deep black pit. Later we were wedged between stones in an icy mountain stream unable to extricate ourselves and slowly freezing to death. Rosa flew overhead like a lovely cherub with a couple of tatters of red ribbon, beseeching us to climb out. She was still wearing my cap. That's how I knew it was a dream.

V

MODERN DON QUIXOTE

IT was a tingling clear morning and instead of working, as I was determined to do, I lingered in the plaza, enjoying the liquid shadows from the ancient walls and ancient ahuehuetes, all old before the Spaniards came—ill-kempt now, but very handsome. The Dominican monastery facing the garden-side plazuela is the third oldest Catholic religious edifice on the American continent. Beside it, behind false pepper trees, is early San Juan Bautista Church and, across from it, Cortés's Palace, older than the two churches, finished in 1522, the seat of Mexico's first Conquest government.

But today a marble slab in the wall reads

HOMAGE TO THE LAST KING . . . CUAHTEMOC.

The last Aztec emperor had his feet roasted in a fire here in Coyoacán to force him to disclose hidden treasure. "This is not a bed of roses," he commented, probably the understatement of that particular year.

In this low, rambling structure, which now houses the town government, Cortés's first wife, Catalina Juárez, died mysteriously. After a shotgun wedding in Cuba, he set out to conquer Mexico and took up with Marina, the brilliant native girl who guided him through his battles and his diplomacy with native caciques, or Indian rulers, and who bore him a son. When Catalina arrived on the scene, Cortés had already married Marina off to one of his obliging captains, but Hernán and his wife did not get along well. The story goes that at a tipsy banquet Cortés accused her before the guests of goings-on with one of her handsome Indian servitors, that there was a royal row. But what is sauce for the gander is not always sauce for the goose. In the morning her body was found at the bottom of the well. Vulgar rumor insisted that the great captain had strangled her and drowned her. The official autopsy is: death by asthma.

Everyday life was still going on in this secluded suburb, much of it still in the pre-Cortés pattern. But folk were now going in and out of the Spanish corner grocery. Its owner, Don Hernán, is a clever, wiry Extremeño, from the same province in Spain as Cortés and bearing the same first name. For four hundred years, all through the life of the colony and the years of the republic, most grocery-store keepers in Mexico, even in villages, have been Spaniards, not Mexicans

—a nation-wide monopoly which has returned to the sons of
the hidalgos total earnings greater than all the plundered
gold of the Indies. So Doña Catalina did not die in vain.

Still reluctant to go indoors, I nosed about the quaint corners of the town. Noon crept up, so I decided to go to Don
Pepe's for lunch—it was Thursday. As usual, spry grandmother Leonor presided in her carved throne of a chair and
kept the table alive with her spicy wit. Playwrights, high
officials, and others were present and, to my delight, my
chess-playing friend, Don Aurelio Manrique, towering up
with his black beard. We exchanged the customary *abrazo*.
As usual, lunch was a series of endless courses and endless
arguments which soon turned into the din of simultaneous
monologues.

The generations, even in Pepe's family, were split between
the old and the new dispensations, pre-Revolution, post-Rev-
olution, feudal versus modern. Miguel, Pepe's eldest son by
his first wife, a chubby replica of Pepe, belonged to the new
order and was still giving the family headaches by threaten-
ing to marry his cantina-girl mistress. Warmhearted Pepe
was of the feudal era, though clever enough to make profitable deals with the government; anyway he loved all human
beings too much to maintain an outraged pose about life or
politics. At the table he humorously poured oil on the roiled
waters when arguments grew too heated.

Don Aurelio, in spite of his pre-Christian Hebraic appearance, was ardently new-eraish, although he usually
managed to be in the losing faction and had just come back
from some years in forced exile. But he was now head of the
National Library, a venerable institution predating anything
in the United States. Few men better typified the noble
extremes of Spanish character: dignity, quick, lofty intel-

ligence, warm impulsiveness, courage. Lovable Don Pepe
was a mestizo, of mixed blood, and symbolized the fuzzy
mixing of races and cultures, the "cosmic" Mexican of the
future, though without the ruthless opportunism that usually characterizes the mixture, for he had been a pampered
son never obliged to fight his way into the sunlight as had
his forebears. But he had the pliant adaptability of the
mestizo, whereas Don Aurelio had the austerity and moral
decisiveness of the old hidalgos, plus vast kindly simplicity.
His gestures were always on the grand order, his ideals
worth dying for whatever the cost, so his deeds were like-
wise epic. His ardor for the common man—individual and
en masse—was ever burning in his tiger-bright eyes. He was
a belated Don Quixote righteously and fervently tilting at
the windmills of social injustice.

I had first met him years back when he was governor of
San Luís Potosí, a north-central desert and mountain state.
Having heard of his unusual program and antics, I smelled
an unusual personality and story, and on an impulse had
gotten off the train to interview him.

Later, when he had fallen from grace and had no money,
I used to play chess with him in Mexico City. His room was
so tiny, he had to pile his great stack of books that reached
to the lofty ceiling on his bed in the daytime and laboriously
restack them on the floor at night. A remarkable scholar,
he could hold his own with experts in any field of knowledge. Though he had never been out of Mexico before that
time, he spoke English, German, French, Russian, and
Italian, and I know not how many other languages fluently.
Then, exiled to the United States, he had vanished into the
great American jungle known as Hollywood.

"What did you do there?" I asked.

He had arrived penniless but soon got parts as a super-numerary in films requiring an authentic black beard, and he had taught Greek.

"It doesn't surprise me you know Greek, but it does surprise me that anybody in Hollywood would wish to study it."

"Ah, my friend, even in the most barbarous societies a few are always eager to learn anything."

"Is Hollywood so barbarous?"

"Ah no, it stands at the pinnacle of modern technical civilization, a pink-and-lavender mouthwash Babylon, hectic, without the graceful, beautiful corruption of a Pompeii, but utterly corrupt, scarcely dedicated to any of the things that make civilization truly great."

"The movies?"

"Technically superb, but pitched to a standard of mediocrity. Truth, beauty, artistry are not aims but merely incidental to cheap emotions that must cater to mass taste, to the box office, not the dignity of man, not his noble dreams. But don't blame the producers. Look elsewhere for the seat of the cancer devouring America—so much splendid power, such pitiful lack of intelligence, such devastating hypocrisy. . . ."

"But I thought you believed in the masses, Don Aurelio."

"In their rights. In safeguarding justice and decency. Not in catering to base traits acquired because of the struggle for survival."

I came back to languages. "If you suddenly began speaking Zulu, Don Aurelio, it wouldn't surprise me." I reminded him of an evening in a café when a central European Jewish refugee came to our table peddling neckties. Don Aurelio struck up a conversation with him in Russian, Polish, German, then intermediary Slavic dialects to pinpoint where he had come from. Afterward he turned to us with pardonable vanity. "How's that?"

"I could follow every word," boasted Pablo Casanova, an anthropologist. He was Aurelio's equal in the command of European languages and was versed in four Mexican Indian languages.

But Don Miguel Mendizábal, another anthropologist, drawled, "You are both quite qualified, I see, to peddle neckties."

"To know many languages is not very remarkable," Don Aurelio observed to me now. "Once you have learned one, the rest come easily. Once the brain has been trained to store up words and syntax, the capacity is limitless. In a lifetime the ordinary brain stores up about fifteen trillion separate bits of information. Thus the storage place for all the vocabularies I know is about one one millionth per cent of my brain capacity. Most people merely store up random bits of information, quiz-program fashion, superstitions, set prejudices. Where nearly all human beings fall down is coordinating and utilizing the facts stored up, in short, *thinking*. Left alone, the brain is merely an automatic parrot speaking back what it has been told. Brain washing is the easiest thing in the world. People always repeat back, like a phonograph disk, what they have heard over the radio or read in the papers or are told by the powers-that-be, and proudly call it *thinking*. Their personal vanity fortifies them in their ignorance. To think requires a definite act of will, and humans are lazy. Only a tiny handful of the man monkeys do any thinking."

After lunch at Don Pepe's we took the interurban into the city to have a game of chess. I suggested we get a board at

Tió Lobo's bar, forgetting that Don Aurelio was a teetotaler. He suggested a little restaurant on Avenida Brasil. When we were seated over a soiled tablecloth in an atmosphere of fried pig's grease and tingling chile, I reminded him how generously he had received me, a stranger, when he had been governor.

I had been seated in the executive antesala, telling myself it was silly, for I knew all the red tape and time wasting required to see Mexican officials even after laboriously arranging an appointment. But presently Manrique's black beard poked through an inner door. "Who's next?" he called. Without the buffer of a secretary Manrique was seeing all-comers, regardless of rank, in the order they had entered his waiting room.

At his call a barefoot Indian woman, with a striped blue *rebozo* framing her brown face, swished in her long skirts into his office, a little goat pattering at her heels. A waiting colonel shifted his pistol and bit his mustache, provoked at being preceded by such rabble. Here waiting were Indians, peasants in sandals, mestizos in cream-colored suits, businessmen, ranchers in embroidered leather jackets. An elegant lady clasped a prayer book. Her black veil indicated the personal concealment required of an aristocratic lady visiting a public office to see a hated politician of the new dispensation.

Later Manrique told me she had come to enlist his good offices in locating a vagabond son, needed at home because the father was infirm, to help save the dwindling family patrimony. Aurelio never turned a deaf ear to any appeal for help.

His first official act as governor had been to cut his meager forty-peso-a-day salary to fifteen pesos. By living in a humble boardinghouse, he was able to give part of even this reduced salary to the needy. Once I saw him smite down an abusive policeman who had overturned the wares of an aged Indian woman who had refused to move on, and I saw him, the governor of the state, get down on his knees in the slimy gutter and pick up her scattered fruit, then, taking her gently by the arm, he carried her load to a location where peddlers were allowed.

Whenever enforcement of the law was dangerous, rather than oblige a subordinate to run the risk, he strapped on a gun and mounted his white horse and personally faced the danger. San Luís Potosí, thanks to him, had a severe prohibition law—to my mind unwise, for it hit a major blow at the state's chief industry, the raising of maguey plants in an arid region where nothing else would grow, for the making of pulque, mescal, and tequila. Few officials had cared to antagonize the powerful liquor interests, and liquor continued to be sold openly. Manrique provided himself with a weird assortment of rusty padlocks and whenever he came upon a saloon he would ride his white charger through the swinging doors and close it down. He was a Mexican Carrie Nation.

One evening late, brooding on humanity's ills and the abuses of his predecessor's office, Manrique wondered how many prisoners had been wrongfully incarcerated. Except for the model federal prison in the capital, the Mexican penal system is antiquated and corrupt. The courts are the tools of the political clique in power. Jails do not rehabilitate, quite the contrary. With Manrique to think is to act. In the wee hours of a freezing winter night he rode down to the state prison, routed out the warden, and ordered all but proven serious offenders brought to the prison patio. He

harangued them henceforth to be law-abiding citizens. The
gates were swung open, and Manrique declaimed, "Go
forth, my sons, you are free!" Something of an anticlimax
resulted when several poor wretches refused to leave because it was cold out and they had no other place to sleep.

Manrique was indefatigable in touring his state, mostly on
horseback with considerable hardship. He went into the
remotest Indian corners, listened to complaints, and tried to
rectify injustices or satisfy demands. Often he rode alone,
telling no one his destination, so local officials would have
no chance to conceal abuses.

Once on his way back to the capital he fell in with a band
of armed men. The leader said they were going to the capital
to seize the governor and hang him.

"Have you ever seen the governor?" Manrique asked.

"No, but they say he has a big black beard like yours."

"I will ride with you," said Manrique. "I'd like to measure
beards with the rascal."

He listened to the reasons for their lawless expedition
and suggested that before they hanged the governor they
call on that gentleman and present their grievances. "They
say he receives everybody. If he is reasonable, you won't
have to hang him. If not, you can seize him on the spot."

Getting to the capital, the leaders went to the executive
offices. When Manrique stepped out, their eyes popped in
their heads. He drew back his coat. "I'm not wearing a gun.
You are free to do with me as you will."

They became numbered among his most ardent sup-
porters.

Indian villages customarily greet all travelers with music.
Once when Manrique was riding along among remote hills
in a poor corner of the state three old Indians rose out of

the rocks and cactus and began singing a quavering song of
welcome. They invited him to their thatched village, almost
invisible among the stones, and fed him as best they could,
for they had little food. They apologized for their meager
hospitality, especially for the shabby music. They were too
poor to buy instruments. As he rode off, his identity not
disclosed, they stood among the rocks singing farewell till
his horse dipped from sight.

Sometime later a string of burros plodded over the hills,
laden with drums, horns, trombones, clarinets, fiddles, bearing the simple words, "From his Excellency, the Governor,
to the hospitable folk of Arroyo Seco. Effective Suffrage and
No Re-election." With the gift came an invitation for the
mayor and three aged musicians to visit him at the capital.
There they were greeted by the military band and seated in
their leather sandals, white pajamas, red sashes, and tousled
black hair at a stately banquet under the capitol dome in
the presence of impeccably dressed state officials.

More than a year later, when Manrique had fallen from
power and was living in his cubbyhole on a back street in
Mexico City, the villagers of Arroyo Seco traveled on foot
more than five hundred miles to serenade and comfort him
in his hour of defeat. Until late at night they played under
his window, slept in the park because they had no money,
and came back at dawn to play mañanitas, those hauntingly
sweet morning songs which once heard in drowsy waking
moments strike deep into the heart and soul never to be forgotten as long as life endures.

Manrique's downfall grew out of a clash with the federal
military commandant, General Saturnino Cedillo, a nasty
ignorant tzar of the Revolution, full of vices and greed,
whose affairs with women were a nation-wide scandal. He

was stealing property and throwing peasants off their lands. Already he was scheming to take over the whole country by force. Fireworks began when Manrique stopped many of his abuses.

President Calles had just said in a public address that Manrique was one of the only two honest loyal governors in the country. But Cedillo was a powerful militarist with troops at his back, and Calles removed Manrique, elected by free vote, by force. The folly of this became visible when the subsequent Cárdenas administration had to put down a serious Cedillo revolt.

Manrique had to pawn his watch to get to Mexico City. Though in exile, betrayed by Calles and opposed by Cedillo, he ran for Congress from San Luís Potosí and, without spending a cent, was elected.

His great idol was President-elect General Alvaro Obregón, but before he could take office the latter was assassinated under Manrique's eyes in the Bombilla Restaurant in San Angel. Aurelio charged violently that his murder was due, not to religious fanaticism, but to a plot by Calles and Labor Tzar Luis N. Morones. Public emotions were so stirred that Morones barricaded himself in the Department of Industry and Labor Building where he was secreted behind machine guns, and Calles was almost tumbled from office.

Calles astutely bowed to public clamor and appointed a police chief satisfactory to Manrique to investigate the crime and called a joint meeting of Congress and army leaders to offer the country more democracy. Even the Catholics were promised religious and political freedom. Actually he was preparing a tight totalitarian party to rule the country, one which to this day has exercised monopoly over all public offices.

At Calles's words Congress rose cheering en masse. Even Ambassador Dwight W. Morrow, in the central guest balcony, forgot protocol, and rose to clap madly. Calles departed with his aides down the long strip of red carpet. Tall Manrique, whose seat happened to be on the aisle, stood arms akimbo, his black beard bristling, a derisive smile on his lips and, as the dictator-president came abreast, the congressman from San Luís Potosí cried out in a ringing voice that echoed to the great dome and back to the marble gold-encrusted panels where were seated all the great generals of the land: *"Farsante! Farsante!"* The cheering died away in confused babble. For a split second Calles's step faltered, then with red fury he passed on out through an assemblage stricken into dour silence.

Manrique was always fearless. At Obregón's mahogany bier he slapped a pet Calles general for not having the decency to remove his pistol when viewing the remains. This general, known as "The Killer," a lean, brutal fellow who had disposed of many prisoners and enemies of the regime by *Ley Fuga*—shooting them in the back—though Manrique was unarmed, slunk out.

After Calles put in a puppet president by rubber-stamp elections Manrique's bitterness caused him to join with the ill-starred Escobar revolt. Escobar, however, was merely a militarist trying to feather his own nest and offered nothing for the peace or progress of the country. The revolt was smashed, Manrique, the last die-hard, led a cornered force in northwest Sonora till obliged to flee into the United States. While still on Mexican soil, he raised his fist against the pursuing federals who dared not fire across the border, and, like a mighty Jeremiah, his black beard shaking in the breeze, shouted, "I shall return."

Now he was back and head of the National Library, and we were playing chess in a dingy restaurant on Brasil Avenue. He was the second best chess player in the country, and he cleaned up the board with a brilliant coup I had never encountered.

"Apparently, Don Aurelio," I told him ruefully, "you didn't spend all your time in Hollywood teaching Greek."

VI

THE JEWELER'S PLUMP WOMEN

"Anchors Aweigh" had sounded. The aroma of coffee drifted out from the charcoal kitchen.

"Petra, tonight we shall have another party."

Her eyes lit up.

"It will be for Don Aurelio, the caballero with the big black beard."

The usual commotion started. Mario had finished sweeping, now he hustled a pail of water to scrub the entrance. María and Lupe set to work scrubbing the flowers with yellow stain that soon colored their hands. Petra clattered loudly in the kitchen.

I sallied forth to get fruit for the punch. Don Nacho's long legs were already across the sidewalk. He knew the saying: The early bird gets the worm. People like to start the day feeling generous. I dropped the usual coin into his peaked sombrero.

Doña Carmen's fruit stand consisted of packing cases labeled "tomatoes" under a tripod awning of patches of burlap and canvas. She sat on a straw *petate*, a mound of bright skirts. Beside her, on the white cloth she wore about her head for sun protection or coiled into a ring to cushion head-carried loads, was her frugal lunch of tortillas, chile, and cheese. Mostly she sold oranges but had a few mounds of puckery cherry-plum fruit, peanuts, chiles, and loose cigarettes for those unable to afford a whole pack. Every morning I bought two oranges from her.

"*Muy buenos días,* Doña Carmen."

"*Muy buenos días,* Caballero."

"You are always alone here, Carmen."

"The children are grown up, señor. Only two. The others died young. God's will, señor."

"Did they have good doctors?"

"What a question! Do the poor ever have doctors?"

"Then it wasn't wholly God's fault, was it?"

"Now the Señor is joking. Since poverty also is God's will. Not everyone can be a great general."

"What are your children doing?"

"My boy works in the city. The girl is married and lives in Puebla."

"Do you hear from her?"

"Every year, señor, on my saint's day. She is happy."

"Your husband, is he living?"

"Thanks to God's blessing, señor. He works at the brick

ovens. He is a good man, señor. Hardly ever does he get drunk."

"Doña Carmen, today I'm going to buy all your oranges."

Amazed, she made me repeat it, then her face darkened and she began to mutter. She shook herself like a setting hen. "Every morning, señor, you buy two oranges, not so? And every morning I save out the two nicest ones, and I keep them for you even though sometimes you do not come by until afternoon. Is that not the truth, señor?"

"Yes, Doña Carmen, you are very kind."

"Well, here they are. And that is all you can have."

"But, Doña Carmen . . ."

She wrapped up the two oranges in a screw of newspaper and handed them to me with fateful finality. I explained I was giving a party.

"Take your two oranges and get along with you before I get really angry."

"But why won't you sell me the rest?"

She shook her feathers and clucked. "And then, pray tell, with all my stock sold, what on earth would I do the rest of the livelong day?"

And so I had to get the rest of my oranges elsewhere.

By nightfall Petra, still breathless, had put on a lace-frilled polka-dot blouse and her dazzling rooster brooch to admit guests through the big double doors. Mario, grinning like a full moon in his snowy communion suit, struggled with wraps and hats. María had gone home grieving with a cold. Shimmering Lupe, a bow in her hair, a spring in her heel, and an unusually saucy sparkle in her eye, served refreshments.

To everyone's disappointment, Don Aurelio never showed up, which surprised me, for he was the soul of punctilious-

ness. But Don Pepe had composed a special poem for the
occasion, so dripping with eulogies, I squirmed. Lesley
Simpson, dean of Spanish at the University of California,
now researching in the archives, produced a special Spanish
ballad and accompanied himself on the guitar, then gave
way to Guty Cárdenas, the famous popular song writer.
Isabel graciously put aside grand opera and sang folk songs
with him. Heliodor Valle, the Honduran journalist later an
ambassador, told yarns with that nervous chuckle of his
that never seemed real. Howard Phillips, editor of *Mexican
Life*, with whom I went horseback riding to the Chapultepec
lomas every week, did magician tricks. Frances Toor, editor
of *Mexican Folkways*, also came. And my darling Delia with
her massed red hair almost too heavy for her slim, graceful
neck, an arrow of sheer delight.

Among those invited were David Saavedra and his sweetheart Mary Grant. He was a roly-poly Spaniard, sleek, perfumed, aglitter with diamonds, who smiled endlessly but
rarely talked. She was a luscious blond angel, plumper than
he, with a sweet babyish face behind severe glasses. They
sat snuggled close together on the couch, holding hands,
beaming fondly at each other. It was an incredible match
no one believed would work.

She was the secretary of an important missionary organi-
zation, he was a free-lance jewelry broker. Revolutionary
days had given him profitable deals with generals and their
mistresses. When a mistress was discarded or needed cash,
Saavedra brought back his jewelry at cut rates and resold it
to the keepers of mistresses at a juicy profit. Now that things
had settled down, his profits were slimmer. He spent as little
as he could these days, except for a while on a Suiza cabaret
girl who cost him a pretty penny. He never stinted on

clothes or personal adornment and was a gourmet, but he begrudged every cent spent on necessities. Since he rarely got up before noon he had to provide himself with only two meals a day. This he solved neatly.

Lunch he had at Mary Grant's apartment, where she lived with her mother, a New England Boston Back Bay aristocrat. Dinner he secured from Harriet Goldman, a striking brunette of about forty, with a Gibraltar bosom and Mount Atlas flanks. Harriet preferred dashing young Latin blades, but David wormed into her good graces. After dinner with her, he always went back to Mary's apartment to spend the rest of the evening, convenient because the two ladies lived within three blocks of each other.

He preferred Mary. She was more refined and innocent. She had devoted her whole life to prayer books and hymns, good deeds, and strait-laced notions. She was hard hit, for belated romance is often the most violent of all, and the idea of remaining a spinster had begun to terrify her. Sweetness had accumulated in her until she was a walking honeycomb, and she was obviously well sexed, but Puritanism had dyked up normal passion until she was a simmering volcano dangerously ready to erupt. The fires buried in her voluptuous body enslaved her emotions far more than was possible in an easygoing French widow like Harriet. All Mary's hopes were centered in this strange, smiling Buddha named David.

She first ran into him when going to her office. She took his eye at once. She had the peaches-and-cream complexion of a girl of sixteen. In her flowered chiffons and her wide, flouncing hats that threw soft shadows on her face she had a luscious, well-washed look. Each time he met her he tilted his hat most gravely.

One cardinal sin was to speak to the Unknown-man-on-the-street. She averted her face, cheeks flaming, bosom a-flutter and arrived at her desk breathless, weakness in her loins, but mornings when she did not run into him made her anxious and unhappy. In a daring moment she gave him a peck of a nod and a smile.

He strolled a few blocks with her. A bit shorter than she was, sleek and shiny, he paced along, chest out, a silk handkerchief spraying out from his pocket, and eyed the world with a confident Olympian smile. He talked only polite chit-chat. To serious topics he always listened with a steady smile, never committing himself.

Mary thought him very foreign, but was impressed by his neatness, his gold-headed cane, and Panama hat. She made discreet inquiries, but none of her American friends had ever heard of him. She invited him to a small buffet party with more Bohemian friends used to associating with Mexicans.

He seemed to enjoy himself, though all he did was sit smiling in the middle of the big sofa, his pudgy bediamonded hands on his fat knees, his legs scarcely touching the floor, and purred steadily like a well-fed tomcat. His eyes scarcely strayed from Mary's soft corpulence and frequently a scarlet wave welled from her deep, curving bosom to the tips of her ears.

Mary's mother, a thin, acidulated D. A. R. Yankee, loathed all things foreign and considered it a disgrace that any Latin ever stepped into the apartment. Picturing David married to Mary and in her Back Bay Boston setting was too awful to contemplate. His immaculate politeness spelled deceit; his dark complexion, for all his lily-white skin, spelled SIN in caps, his inability to speak English, (she knew only six words of Spanish and mispronounced them atrociously), branded him as an ignoramus; his glittering diamonds marked him as a man of vulgar tastes. Later we learned he had a profound knowledge of literature, painting, and music about which Mrs. Grant knew nothing. All she owned in life were property and prejudices—and Mary.

It was a torture for her to have him at lunch every day. In the evening, she felt it her duty to be a stern, watchful chaperone, but was so outraged she always went to her room with a sick headache. Mary was thunderstruck at the amount he ate, but the meals were a relief after facing the prim gloom of her mother for so long.

Mrs. Grant wailed, "Must we have that awful perfume shop here every meal?"

"Mother," protested Mary, more emphatically than she had ever dared, "I'm old enough to choose my own friends. In this climate a few gentlemen I might name, not Latins either, could imitate him."

"Better if he took a bath."

Daggers struck from Mary's eyes; she never felt the same toward her mother again.

Thrilled by his polite deference, Mary tingled at every ardent glance. From his large, dark eyes deep mystery welled up from a way of life strange to her. Sometimes she felt physically mussed and was shocked to discover she enjoyed it. He always kissed her hand, and little ripples ran through her flesh and splashed against her tingling spine and curled sweetly about her breasts. With an enormous feeling of guilt, she wondered how it would feel if he kissed her—his lips were so full and sensuous.

Whenever he came late, she felt sick and miserable. One night he did not come. Utterly forlorn, she imagined

terrible things happening to him and could not sleep. But
when he appeared for lunch next day, she was so relieved
she could not scold him. He explained elaborately that a beloved uncle of his had been ill. He kissed her good night.

Her legs became so weak she could hardly get to her
bedroom. She hugged her body in sweet anguish, and her
lips flamed for hours.

Mrs. Goldman was merely puzzled and irked by David's
polite restraint. He always extricated himself gracefully
from the eloquent opportunities she gave him.

David became engaged to both Harriet and Mary at the
same time. Marriage was more than Harriet wanted but she
soon grew enamored of the idea. Mary was in seventh
heaven. He stalled them both on engagement rings, saying
that in his business something choice was bound to turn
up. He congratulated himself warmly on this admirable
method of guaranteeing himself excellent home-cooked
meals.

Mary, blooming with rapture, kept the news from her
mother. One afternoon at a large tea she overheard Mrs.
Cole, wife of a road contractor, say in a chirpy voice, "Have
you seen Mrs. Grant's roly-poly friend? A Spaniard, I believe. The scandal is, he's also engaged to that Harriet Goldman. Too droll for words. . . ."

Mary prickled hot and cold. She wanted to tell Mrs. Cole
to hold her gossipy tongue, except she had just donated five
hundred pesos to Mary's charity work.

Being a forthright person, Mary told David what she had
heard. He put his plump hand to his heart and swore that
Mrs. Goldman was merely teaching him English, and to
demonstrate his progress said, "For my beautiful Mary, all
my affections are in the bull's eye for always." She fell into

his arms with a solidity that rocked him on his heels. "Don't worry, my little flower," he said.

She leaned back from him, searching his face. "I also heard you went to Cuernavaca with some officers and ladies, but you gave me another reason for not coming that day."

He stroked her soft cheek. "My darling, I had to accept a last-minute engagement. In my jewelry business I can't afford to offend important contacts. Besides, one so lovely as you is always worthy of the most imaginative prevarications."

Mary gasped at this challenge to her ideas of rigid truth. That poetry could be, perhaps, more truthful than true or more desirable was world shaking. She thought of Keats:

"Beauty is truth, truth beauty—that is all
Ye know on earth, and all ye need to know."

She believed jealousy to be unworthy, but she hated Mrs. Goldman every time she saw her in the Imperial. David simply could not be interested in that hag, but rumors kept coming to her ears. She passed sleepless nights, then girt up her loins in her best gown over a new streamlined girdle and bra she had recently bought blushingly and went straight to the tearoom.

Mrs. Goldman came over, a trifle hostile, to take her order. Mary toyed with the salt shaker. "People have been bringing me terrible tales. They concern Señor Saavedra."

Mrs. Goldman's black smudge eyebrows lifted. "Ah, yes . . ."

"He and I have been engaged for four months . . ."

"Engaged to you!" squealed Harriet. "Oh, Miss Grant . . ." She clasped her thick hands near her throat. "Impossible!

He's engaged to me! It's the silliest thing I ever heard!"

Their hostility watered down to dismay. Mary was crushed. "He comes to my house every day."

Harriet's nose edged up. "He comes to my house every evening for dinner, and he tells me he loves me."

Mary's heart churned to jelly. "He tells me the same."

"The scoundrel!" ejaculated Harriet.

"He isn't."

"He certainly is."

Each thinking by rights he's mine, I intend to keep him, Mary suggested they confront him together. Mrs. Goldman clasped her hands at her throat again and invited Mary to dinner. "And then . . ."

"And then we'll get at the truth."

She arrived breathless half an hour early. The stodgy front room, with its threadbare carpet and Vera Cruz shell curtains, the kind tourists buy, smelled of varnish and wax lilies. The two women sat nervously on the edge of the frayed upholstered chairs. Both were a bit hysterical. The clock ticked on and on. David did not show up. A tiny smile of triumph roosted on Mary's soft face.

"He always comes," declared Harriet defensively.

An hour late they sat down to the meal, barely poking at the food. "The wretch!" Harriet wailed. They wept into their soup and ended up sobbing in each other's arms. Both swore they would have nothing more to do with the bounder. Claimed by this momentous decision, they told each other the details of their intimacies. The theme of David proved inexhaustible.

Mary rose to leave, thinking hopefully that David would surely show up at her place. Shamed by her unworthy hope, which Harriet instantly suspected, she suggested the latter come over. "I want to avoid any scene in front of Mother, but most likely she'll be in bed."

They sat stiffly in Mary's parlor. Ten-thirty rolled around. "He's smelled a rat," said Harriet. The doorbell rang. They looked at each other wildly.

A messenger handed Mary a message: "Mary, my true love, my uncle is dreadfully ill again. Many kisses, David."

Mary handed it over. "Just read that!"

"The wretch! He hasn't got an uncle. Kisses! The sneak! How dare he write like that!"

"And why shouldn't he?" flared Mary.

They looked at each other helplessly, tears oozing down their noses. Harriet blubbered that she was leaving. Too nervous to sleep, Mary walked her home. They covered the three blocks falteringly and clung to each other miserably. Telling their stories over and over, they made four trips back and forth at an hour when respectable ladies never went abroad in Mexico City. A taxi sped down the street. In it was David.

Both women screamed at him, but the taxi sped on. They tore down the street after it, shouting. The Great God of Irony never had a more hilarious opportunity: two buxom foreign ladies racing down the street in the dead of night after a flying auto and shouting at the top of their lungs. The car turned into a blind *callejón*, a narrow dead-end street, where David lived. When they dashed around the corner, he was already fitting his key into the door.

"David! David!" they yelled, but he ducked inside and slammed the door.

They pounded furiously, crying to him to open. Windows along the street began going up. Frowsy heads poked out.

If the story had ended at this ludicrous point, as everyone expected, it would be too cruel and pointless to relate.

Mary was a wreck for a week, then swallowed her pride and wrote David an affectionate note, ending, "I will always love you, no matter what you do." Her friend Kate, to whom she showed it, said to tear it up and forget him. Kate, an Irish girl working in a government bureau, knew more about Latin males than Mary would ever know. But cyclones cannot be diverted by friendly advice.

That night a sheepish David showed up. He sat on the couch, his arm around her ample waist, and swore he cared only for her. He showed her a letter to Harriet breaking off with her and thrust it into Mary's hands to mail. She tucked it back in his pocket, saying she would always trust him. They could not get enough of kissing after that.

At least he had saved his noonday meal. Also, he was jolted into realizing that he loved Mary deeply. Harriet was damaged goods, but Mary was an unspoiled peach, and her devotion beyond earthly measurement. She promised new rewarding experience. But there were problems. He told her that free-lance jewelry selling was no longer lucrative, they would have to wait until he got into something steady.

"What would you like to do?" she asked.

"I'd like to set up a money-exchange place on Isabel la Catolica. One can make lots of money that way without much work. But I've never been able to scrape enough together to swing it."

"We'll do it now!" cried Mary. "I've a few thousands saved up."

David was touched, and they made plans. "Your mother can live with us," he said generously, though he hated her like poison, and he added in English, "She like not me, and I like not she, but I'm the polite person always and never trouble come between us. Always I tell her the nicest lies she cannot hold more than the fog."

But Mary said her mother would be glad for an excuse to go home. "Anyway, it's high time I lived my own life." The marriage date was set. Mary and her mother went to the States. Mary packed up her furniture there and shipped it to Mexico and liquidated the stocks and bonds in which her money was invested. Her mother wept that she was making a tarnation fool of herself. All Mary's friends thought she was being taken for a cleaning. She told Kate, when she got back to Mexico, that the only basis for a marriage was generosity and trust. If things turned out badly, what, then, was the loss of her money when all would be lost?

David set to work at once getting the new business started. He was so busy he missed many engagements and made her heart ache, and her friends worried. But to watch them holding hands at my party, they were two lovesick birds, David as much as she.

In spite of Don Aurelio's absence our party was a big success. Larry Mason came late. He was so shy he could never talk to a woman without blushing. But tonight—I suspected a few prior drinks—he bounded in hilariously and ran around the room and put everybody's drink down with a gulp. Since different kinds had been served, the combination was dynamite. Larry boldly made love to every woman present. Mona, a Dominican girl, staved him off cleverly. I was wondering how David would react. Larry dropped on his knees before Carmen Mendizábal, wife of my anthropologist friend, and covered her hands with kisses. This was hard for a Latin husband to take, and Miguel, who always carried a gun, strode over menacingly.

He held out, not his gun, but two pesos in silver. "Go buy yourself a woman," he said grossly.

Larry folded up, his face crimson, and sat silent in a corner the rest of the evening.

Petra rushed in, excited. "The musicians have arrived."

"What are you babbling about?" I hastened to the door.

Five tall Guadalajara Indians in white pajamas and battered straw sombreros stood there, clutching their instruments, an itinerant Mariachi orchestra. The leader handed me a letter embossed Biblioteca y Archivos Nacionales Mexicanos. It was from Don Aurelio.

On setting out for our party, a bunch of pro-Nazi hoodlums had seized him and cut off his beard. He was not otherwise injured, but the disgrace of it prevented him from showing himself in public till his beard grew out again. He hoped I would not be provoked and as compensation was sending out his favorite Mariachi orchestra.

It is typically Mexican to think of others in the midst of one's own adversity.

The Mariachi players kept our party going until the small hours. The lovebirds on the couch came out of their trance and cornered me. Mary was six shades of pink. David, too, was embarrassed. Would I be a witness at their wedding?

I groaned. All that rigmarole again—boring visits to dingy government offices, papers to sign, things to swear to; this time worse, for there was also a church wedding, visits to the priest, and more papers.

"On one condition," I told David, "that I can kiss the bride now and at the wedding."

I folded Mary's ripe softness into my arms, and she gave me her fruity mouth. I knew then, for sure, David had made a good bargain.

VII

THE BOHEMIANS COME

APPARENTLY I had slept through my neighbor's "Anchors Aweigh," for I woke to the oompety-oomp of his setting-up exercises: "*Uno . . . dos . . . tres . . . Uno . . . dos . . . tres. . . .*" I bounded into the sunlight and headed for the corral to take my splash.

María was already slapping clothes. "There's a fiesta in town," she said.

Rockets were popping in the sky in noisy succession.

"There's a Ferris wheel . . . and booths . . . and music . . . and . . ."

"Fine! I'll stake you to a few rides."

This was going to be a busy day. First, Fernando Gon-
zález was coming over with documents about his grandfather, Manuel, who had been president in the eighties and
who had left office clouded by scandals of corruption. Instead of living his own life, Fernando spent all his energies
delving into musty records to clear his grandfather's reputa-
tion, with typical Mexican obsession for the sacred family.
But Fernando failed to show up.

I phoned his home. His wife said he had gone to see a man
who had promised to pay a back debt.

When Fernando came the following day, he gave me the
most elaborate romantic cock-and-bull yarn I have ever
heard as to why he had not kept his engagement.

"And did you collect your money?" I asked drily.

Somewhat deflated, he said haughtily, "It would be an
insult to you had I broken our engagement because of mere
money matters."

White lies in Mexico are not white lies, they are beautiful
fairy tales. Sometime after this Fernando lost a leg fighting
for Franco in Spain. That, too, was a fairy tale, for it identi-
fied him more closely with his heroic grandfather who had
lost an arm fighting the French.

But my pretty typist, Matilda, showed up this morning
of the village fiesta right on time with material I had asked
her to copy from mid-century newspapers. She always fished
out some amusing morsel to tell me. Today it was an old
item about the laying of the first transoceanic cable.

> From a usually reliable New York source, it has been
> reported that a wire cable has been successfully laid
> across the Atlantic and that people have talked over it.
> In keeping with the honest policy of this paper, we give

our readers all information received, but it is only fair to warn everybody that this is an absurd and outright lie.

I invited her to tea at Sanborn's the following week. She colored and said, would I mind coming to her home for tea. I had stepped full-hoofed on another Mexican convention. It was all right for her to come unchaperoned to my house in the line of duty, but to be seen alone with me in public would be shamelessly improper.

Charley Nutter of the Associated Press and his handsome auburn-haired wife Eleanor were coming to lunch. They brought along their bull-terrier puppy, Dick. The animal was a caution. He ran off with everything loose and buried it. During the time I lived in Coyoacán, I dug up from the garden two pipes, a leather tobacco pouch, shoes, slippers, gloves, a shoehorn, even a small Zapotec sandstone idol. Dick had already caused a five-thousand-peso lawsuit.

The Nutters lived in a roof apartment in the center of town. An Irish neighbor, a free-lance oil speculator, loved to tease the puppy. He discovered that Dick hated flit as much as he loved slippers, so Mike would lay the flit gun on top of Dick's play slipper, and the poor pup would bark himself sick. Next, the Irishman bought a smooth knuckle-bone larger than the puppy. Dick nosed it and licked it, but could never get his teeth into it. He wailed, whined, and barked at it helplessly for hours. Finally Mike brought Dick a live turtle. Provoked and mystified at the way the turtle drew out of sight, Dick nosed it all over the roof, barking furiously and hopelessly until fit for a psychoanalyst. The poor turtle finally escaped into a drainpipe. It overflowed into a dress shop below, ruining expensive gowns. The Frenchwoman who owned the establishment, a chic, hand-

some widow, sued the Irishman. Mike made ardent love to
her and, after the second batch of orchids and a few kisses
in the moonlight, she called the suit off, whereupon he went
blithely whistling on his way.

For tea, after the Nutters left, I went to Zelia Nuttal's
place, a few blocks up the avenue, the old Pedro de Alvaro
Palace, built by Cortés's famous lieutenant right after the
Conquest. Its beautiful inner patios and gardens, with rare
exotic flowers and shrubs, the arcades, fountains, and rows
of carved columns made it an architectural gem. It was
packed with old idols, rare codices, pottery, colonial paintings, and furniture, a thousand treasures, more a museum
than a home. Zelia was an amateur archaeologist and had
published scientific treatises on the Aztec calendar.

Until I came she had been the only foreigner living in
Coyoacán; now we were being invaded. A young American
painter, a divorcée, rented the house next to mine on Ave
María. She was a honey blonde, beautiful as sin but a go-
getter to be handled with care, this side up. She had gone to
New York at sixteen to study art and had been taken up by
a famous illustrator who taught her more than she could
ever learn in class. She toiled faithfully for him, tracing out
his designs for long, backbreaking hours far into the night,
scrubbing, ironing, washing his socks. Though she had become a fine painter technically, it was not difficult to trace the
source of her imitative compositions.

She married a Jewish Communist and posed to his rich
family as a bona-fide Jewess until the strain got her down,
then she fled. Her original patron, the illustrator, serving as
a scholarship juror, by astute trading, had gotten her a
scholarship, though she was only nineteen and regulations
said she had to be twenty-five.

She ate at my house for a few days until she got her housekeeping arrangements set up, and presently had a succession of girls to whom she gave board and lodging and taught painting. They adored her hysterically and paid her well. What irritated me most was the way they weaned María away from my establishment, although I was glad to see her earn something.

The day I came back from Zelia's, Petra came to me daubing at her eyes with her apron. "They've had María arrested, señor. But we are honest folk . . ."

I hurried next door. The police were there, scowling at María and taking down data. María was accused of stealing a silk dress and some trinkets.

I made them show me where the silk dress had been hung. I made them look everywhere. I looked myself. How did they know María had taken it?

They were vague. An outside thief, they argued, would have taken all their dresses.

In the back of my head I nursed an unpleasant recollection. About a month before, I had laid my wrist watch on a stack of newspapers beside my desk. The next morning, after María cleaned up, it was gone. I searched every corner. Now María was on the spot.

Badly frightened, sobbing, too incoherent to deny anything, the poor kid was dragged off to the police station in the Cortés Palace, where she was held for days and given a rough going over, physically and mentally, even the rubber-hose treatment. The police also searched Petra's little shack but found nothing. In the end María was released for lack of evidence.

"Where is María?" I ask Petra, for she had not showed up since the trouble.

"She's too shamed to face anybody. Just sits home and cries. She keeps asking whatever will the Señor think of me?"

"Tell her I think she's wonderful, and I know she wouldn't touch a pin."

I bought her a pair of silk stockings to supplement the cheap cotton ones she always wore. I had often scolded her for her sloppy appearance, but she always said, "I'm so bad-looking, what does it matter?" She felt twice the ugly duckling because Lupe was so pretty and vivacious. But my praise whenever she did take some care of her person seemed to do a bit, and, when Gabriel was expected, she perked up and put a flower in her hair.

She dragged in, twisting her dress, a sullen, beaten expression on her face. She put her apron over her head and began blubbering. Like most of her people, apparently so stolid and secretive, she had deep feelings and was supersensitive. I put my arm around her and wiped away her tears. She buried her face in my chest. "Ay, señor. Ay, señor," she wailed. When I undid the package of stockings, she really drowned me.

The next day she showed up dressed like a Chrstmas tree in rayon and shiny new pumps, her hair, the one nice feature about her, carefully arranged with glittering combs. Blushing violently, she lifted her skirts and showed me the silk stockings. But not even silk stockings improved her misshapen underpinnings. She brought me a ripe pineapple, knowing I was fond of pineapple.

Several days later the girls next door found the lost dress under a coat in a spare storage closet. One by one the mislaid trinkets reappeared. I said they should go to the police station and clear María's name. They shrugged. "She's only a servant. She's free, so what does it matter?"

About a week later, when I was digging near the bougain-villaea vine, I turned up my lost wrist watch. Nutter's pup Dick had been the criminal.

Other newcomers whom I helped get settled in Coyoa-cán were Walter Bailey, the Kansas City painter, his wife, and sister-in-law. Both girls were dainty and dazzling, always marcelled to perfection, always exquisitely dressed, as if they had just stepped out of a *Vogue* advertisement, but Walter was always raffish in a battered hat and a rakish gleam in his eye. His painting was unusually good, though it seemed always to come out as marcelled as his pretty wife. He did try at times to put in a few modernistic touches, but without much feeling in that direction. The four of us had fun together, eating around, taking trips to the Teotihua-cán pyramids, and Churriguerresque churches, visiting the markets and out-of-the-way village fiestas.

Presently around the corner, in Marta's house, two more Americans moved in. Marta and Antonio, who had been given the inheritance, had moved to the new fashionable Colonia del Valle subdivision where they had started a store, and Marta's mother was now living with her eldest son and wife. The new renters were a tutor and a college boy, said "boy" being a hulking six-feet-plus football player. In his freshman year, between football and beer busts and failing in half his courses, he had dashed off a novel that hit the best-seller lists. The publishers wanted another script right away, so his wealthy father had hired the tutor to take him to a foreign land where he would see no cronies and hog-tie him to a typewriter.

The tutor, an ex-Marine, who had fought Sandino in Nic-aragua, proudly claimed to be the original of the character in Hemingway's *The Sun Also Rises* injured in the world war

and rendered impotent, though he claimed the damage
had not been that devastating. Intellectually on the precious side, he dabbled in recondite ivory-tower poetry, but he
did introduce me to Jeffers' poems and Faulkner's fiction,
both exciting discoveries.

The hulking football hero who grunted rather than con-
versed pounded his typewriter at the barred front window
where Marta had often sat. He plunked himself there in his
pajamas or an undershirt, a derby hat cocked on his head,
a big cigar in his mouth, and a bottle of beer, a startling
spectacle for Coyoacaners, especially Indians, and a curious
throng always gathered to gape at him for hours.

It made him rage. "Haven't those idiots enough gumption
to go about their business? Why do they have to annoy
me?" Several times he yelled at them furiously in English
to "beat it." This merely provoked hilarity and increased his
audience. "You'd think I'm an animal in a cage," he stormed.

"You are. No one in Coyoacán has ever seen a derby hat,
let alone anybody wearing such headgear and smoking a
cigar before he's dressed and sitting at a typewriter in full
public view. You're a seven days' wonder."

"But I can't think sitting in the back patio looking at a
blank wall. I have to see the street. And I can't think at all
unless I have my derby on and am smoking," he wailed.
"They must be simple-minded creatures."

"Suppose an Indian in a big sombrero and a crimson sash
set up his hand loom in the street window of a small Indiana
town."

"A typewriter isn't a hand loom."

"For some here it's a fascinating foreign gadget never before seen that makes magic words."

Several other writers and artists I did not meet settled

briefly in Coyoacán, but the only other American I ran into, except for tourists with kodaks and Terry's red guide, or Frances Toor's guide, was a down-and-outer named Boak Daggit, who lived in some corner and survived it was hard to tell how. He claimed to be working on some revolutionary kind of mapmaking. Occasionally he hit me for a handout; once I bought him a meal in the little oilcloth Indian restaurant near the plaza and listened to his story.

Why he had drifted into Mexico I was not sure, except he had been jilted by a sweetheart. He'd gone broke in Guanajuato, the silver town, not enough to pay his bill at the Buena Vista Hotel. He had sat in the balcony looking at the tilted street and the achingly blue sky, wondering what the devil to do. Two peons squatted drowsily in the shadow of a rose-tinted wall. They had no problem. Life just was, dawn and noon and night, the sun flowing through their brown bodies. Boak said he wished he could feel carefree like those Mex, not give a damn, not worry, just exist. "But I'm doomed to think, think, think, a goddamn Hamlet, a goddamn Buddha staring at my belly button."

He put on two sets of underwear, two pairs of socks, stuffed another pair in his pocket and a small Spanish-English dictionary inside his shirt. It was hot, he was itchy as a stuffed goose. He sneaked out of the hotel and spent almost his last peso on fare to Celaya.

Getting off the train, he slipped and sliced the upper of his right shoe on something sharp. The irony made him laugh. Seventy centavos in his pocket, and a torn shoe on his foot. He sat in the plaza near the tall Independence monument trying to make up his mind whether to get his shoe fixed or get something to eat.

Down a side street he found a restaurant sign—El Tripoli

—a dirty hole, dingy walls, cheap native green-glass water bottles, grimy paper flowers (in a land of flowers), flies, snooping curs to kick away. A fat, jovial Indian girl served Boak a *comida corrida* for sixty centavos: dishwater soup, rice with tomatoes and chile. Not very filling, and he had to blow through his mouth. He lit his last Buen Tono cigarette and tossed the crumpled cream wrapper into a corner and sat picking his teeth and staring at the plump waitress.

She flung him a flirtatious glance and when she cleared the table he felt of her. She ran off giggling. Just a tub, he thought, but nice to have even a dumb cluck like her smile at him.

He drifted back to the shady old plaza. Twilight descended with swift glides and a faint buzzing. The place filled up with promenaders, caballeros in one direction, señoritas in the other, round and round, the age-old game of hearts. With his torn shoe and empty pocket he felt like a fool outcast. He walked around town, staring into open doorways at the tiles and garden patios. His dogs ached. He ached all over with loneliness. Hownhell would he ever get out of this jam? He trudged back to the center and slept all night in the plaza. Fragile insects, falling from a high arc light, made a ring about him.

He woke stiff and cold, hair and lashes fuzzy with dew. He'd never been so hungry. He walked past Carmen church to the outskirts and lay down in the sun beside an old stone bridge across the Rio Laja. Indian boys came and talked. It was nearly four when he wandered half-famished back to the plaza. At a flour mill near the tracks he asked for work and was turned down. By chance he passed El Tripoli. The plump waitress, dressed up for the afternoon, stood at the doorway.

"Why didn't you come to eat today?" she asked.

He eyed her ample bosom. "I gave my last ten centavos to you for a tip."

"No!" she exclaimed compassionately. "Mother is out, she goes away every afternoon to sew. I'll give you something."

She pulled him to the kitchen and gave him hot stew, tortillas, beans, and coffee. She told him he would have to duck out in a hurry if her mother came back. Her name was Conchita—Little Shell.

"Why is it you have no money?" she asked him.

"I lost my job in Guanajuato," he told her.

"Never mind," she said cheerfully. "Until you find something to do, come here every afternoon."

He put his arm around her and squeezed her. When her black eyes smiled at him, he kissed her. She ducked her head, giggling, but pretty soon kissed him back hard.

Days passed. Boak loafed in the plaza, walked out across the Laja, and slept on the grassy bank; watched the loaded burros jog by. Let the sun seep into him, trying to be unconcerned. Like the Mex. Once or twice he tried to get something to do. "Fat chance in a burg like that, a foreigner scarcely knowing the language." He'd have to figure some way to breeze on. Hop a freight maybe. But for now he could get by on Conchita's food.

He did earn a few pesos one day helping unload a freight car. He blew it on a necklace and earrings for Conchita. There in the kitchen every day, between bites, he hugged her and felt her all over. He talked her into meeting him at night in the cornfield back of the restaurant.

She came in a black tapalo shawl drawn closely about her face, held in place by her two bare arms crossed over her breast, her long brown fingers tapering against her shoulders. It gave her a sweet Madonna look. He grabbed her and pulled her to the ground. Oblivious to the prods of dead stalks, they lay against the odorous moon-dappled earth.

Boak found a dilapidated shack to sleep in, got a petate, and an old sarape for cold nights. Every day he bathed in the river. The water was shallow, full of clay, but it was the best he could do. So he drifted along. He was eating, wasn't he? He had nice hot tail, didn't he? And so slow poison mounted through his blood, the will fiber slackening, the mind cells growing flabby. Sooner or later he would breeze, get to Mexico City. But there wasn't any hurry, not with Conchita's grub and Conchita crazy for him out in the cornfield.

Neighbors' tongues wagged, and one morning, on the pretext of going to Mass, Conchita rushed out to look for Boak. Sobbing from a violent scene with her mother, she warned him not to come to the restaurant any more. But she kept meeting him in the cornfield. Each time she brought him food concealed in her shawl. Finally her visits stopped.

For a time he met her in Carmen church. In the dim little Chapel of Judgment they held hands, occasionally risked a kiss. They knelt together. She would slip him a package of food. But he sure missed those nights in the cornfield.

Finally she could no longer meet him even in church. Several times he passed El Tripoli. She waved and smiled yearningly. He was so hungry several times that he sneaked into cornfields and stole corn to roast. But soon the fields were dry and crackling.

Boldly he went to Conchita's mother and offered to marry the girl. She was a big fat Indian woman with a wise wrinkled face. She grinned at him, though her crafty eyes told him she was damned sore at him. He said he'd help keep things shipshape around her place. Sometime, he thought, I'll breeze, get back to the life I know. Conchita's mother knew that, too. She sent him packing.

It made him sore as a boil. A brown wench like Conchita and her watermelon-belly mother ought to be glad to get a white man. He hoped to hell Conchita would have a kid. Serve them both right. He caught the next freight south.

Here he was in Coyoacán, a lost bum. He had poetry in his make-up, the way he told things and felt things, but it added up to nothing good or useful. There was no way I could help him. He'd have to figure things out for himself, if he could.

After that meal he found out where I lived, and whenever he was in bad straits he would hit me up for a peso or two. He became such a pest, I told Petra always to say I wasn't home.

But one day he shouldered past her roughly and marched into my study and bawled me out for saying I wasn't home. He was so burly and menacing that Petra waited tensely, ready to dash out for the police. Boak roared that he needed some money. As a fellow American it was up to me to see that he didn't starve to death here in this lousy foreign country. He had been drinking. He had money enough for that.

I ordered him out, and when he didn't budge I got up and faced him. He gave ground, and I kept backing him to the door. There I handed him a peso and told him to keep away; next time I'd call the police.

He left, calling me foul names and evidently marched straight to the post office and wrote me an insulting postcard, calling me a liar, skinflint, and cheap skate. He didn't send the peso back.

I sat down irritably to lunch. Petra shoved something

resembling stewed squash at me. It was utterly insipid. "What in heaven's name is this?" I asked.

"Don't you recognize it? That's chayote." She grinned. "I thought you'd be pleased, you were so fond of it."

"Don't ever try it again. Have Mario clean the vine out. It's done for."

Mario got scores of dark green fruit, large as pumpkins, and stacked them against the charcoal shed. Petra said if I put them on the roof, they would keep indefinitely.

"Take the stupid things away."

"You mean, señor, we can have them?" She clasped her hands as though a rich uncle had died.

"Leave me one, a nice large one."

It took Mario until after dark, and brushes with jeering neighbor kids, to lug all those tasteless imitation pumpkins around the corner to Petra's place. The one I saved out I scooped out and made a jack-o'-lantern. Mario, who had never seen this done before, had a lot of fun chasing kids all over town with it.

That night the electric light went off, and I sat out in the kitchen. The charcoal fire and the lone candle threw eerie dancing shadows on the walls and ceilings. The conversation turned to ghosts and the supernatural. It was easy to believe anything in that dim, flickering room. The shadows became monsters, spirits, ogres. I suddenly realized how much of the world's superstition Mr. Edison's tungsten lights had driven into the corners, and with them went many primitive fears, maybe, too, a bit of the world's poetic imagination.

VIII

MAGDALENA MOVES IN

FORTUNATELY, when Petra burst in, I already had my briefs on. She stood twisting her apron. Would the Señor mind, would it be too much imposition, if a friend stayed at the house for a few nights? "There's so much room," she said hopefully.

My thoughts were elsewhere. I was already late for a breakfast appointment at Sanborn's. "Quite all right, Petra."

After breakfast I went up to the Palace where Diego Rivera was mounted on a scaffolding, the boards sagging under his two-fifty-pounds plus, his revolver beside him, painting his latest frescoes. I megaphoned up that I was

99

bringing an American stage director and his sister to lunch.

An American girl was gazing up. She was not looking at the painting but at Diego, with the most adoring expression ever seen on a female's face. Given Diego's froglike structure, it was incredible. She leaned over and kissed his leather jacket lying on a rung of the ladder.

"Would you like to meet him?"

She came out of a dream trance, blushed violently, and fled.

Diego lived in an old section beyond the Palace. We found other guests there, drinks being served. Apparently Diego had neglected to tell Lupe, his wife, that we were coming, for her face registered irritation, and her remarks were so unfriendly that I was glad my friends understood no Spanish. The nerve, she said, of some people barging in at mealtime uninvited.

Lupe had a genius for insulting everybody. She was an untamed creature. Most people liked her tart tongue, calling it "Lupe's way," but today it got under my skin.

Fortunately Diego was delighted with my guests. I whispered to them that I had to leave but Diego wanted them to stay on for lunch. Making some excuse to leave for a few seconds, I slipped out quietly and never returned.

Probably I was too sensitive, for when I ran into Lupe on the street some weeks later she scolded me for having taken French leave, but said, laughing, she supposed I must have run into a pretty girl so she did not blame me. If she had known whom I ran into that afternoon she would have been as surprised as I was.

When I walked into my house I bumped into a four-year-old girl. I presumed it was some child with Petra, though Petra was rarely around at that hour. Glancing up, I saw an elegantly gowned girl, standing on the balcony corridor. She pushed out her clothes with ripe fullness.

In a low, throaty voice, not the usual high-pitched parrot tone of most Mexican women, she introduced herself as Magdalena Manzanares. "I hope I'm not intruding. Petra said I might stay here for a few nights."

I gulped not merely once. Not till then did I recall what Petra had asked me that morning. Whatever is in her head, I thought, that she would bring an unattached beauty like this into a bachelor's home? And how was it that the stunning creature had walked into my den so calmly?

"My little girl won't be any bother," she added.

"There are times when one wishes to be bothered," I replied gallantly. "This is one of those times. I presume, however, that Petra told you that I live here alone."

"Oh, yes," the vision replied easily, "but Petra is here."

"Not exactly. She sleeps in her own place around the corner."

The girl was quite cheerful about it. "That is sufficient, isn't it?"

I did some more gulping. "Is there anything you need? Has Petra attended to everything? . . . Then please make yourself at home." I retreated to my study to mull over the problem of having this luscious morsel under my rooftree. And what was Castanets going to say about it if she found out?

Later, going to the rear of the house, I passed the door of the room where Petra had installed the girl and saw a lot of silk undergarments laid out on the bed.

When Petra came to prepare dinner, Magdalena went out to the kitchen, so I had no chance to make inquiries. When Petra called me to eat, the table was set only for me.

"And our guest? Where is she?"

"The little girl has already had her supper, and Magdalena will eat in the kitchen."

"Tell her I would feel most inhospitable and unhappy eating alone."

And so it was that the strange fair lady came to my table. "This," I remarked, "strikes me as manna from heaven."

She smiled sadly. "If you wish it that way, señor. I am scarcely in a position to object."

Now what the devil did she mean by that speech? I stared at her diamond and her wedding ring. Though her hands looked as if she had been doing hard work, they were perfectly manicured.

Over the coffee she leaned back and looked around. "You could make this place quite attractive. Apparently Petra does not have much knack in that direction." She examined the curtains on the glass doors opening on the patio, and I examined her trim legs, wide hips, and handsome shoulders. "Why, these curtains are only pinned together, not even sewn!" she exclaimed.

Young lady, you are getting a bit nosy, I thought. The eternal instincts of a woman. "You can't expect me to sew," I retorted. "It's bolt stuff I picked up in the market. I just tacked it up."

I got a chance at Petra before she cleared out for home. Magdalena was putting her child to bed. "What in the name of all the saints does this mean?" I demanded.

"Please don't be angry, señor, for you are good of heart."

"You'd be surprised at the state of my heart at this minute. The creature is ravishing."

Petra smiled, very pleased.

"But confound it, tell me how this happened. And why?

What am I supposed to do? How am I supposed to act?"

Petra explained that Lupe used to work for Magdalena when she had her own home. Then she had trouble with her husband and things broke up. "Last night she came to my place weeping. She had no money, no place to stay. She was actually hungry—señor—and with a sweet little girl. It is all right for people like us to be hungry, but not a real lady like her. She stayed at our place last night, but is she the sort who should sleep on a straw mat? You have looked at her. She's not, is she?"

"No, she's the feather-bed type, no doubt of that."

"So I thought, since there is plenty of room here and a nice bed no one is using, it would be all right for a few nights till she can arrange things."

"Just what is she going to arrange?"

"She has put an ad in the paper for work, señor, and God is merciful always. The trouble is for her to find work where people won't mind her little girl, for if she has to she will take work as a servant, though she's not that sort. But she is very brave, and she was always nice to Lupe."

"Doubtless all will be well," I said lamely.

"It is such a shame, señor. Her husband . . ."

I squeaked with dismay. "Yes, her husband . . . That's perfectly fine. Probably in the dead of night he'll tear in here brandishing his pistol or a butcher knife and cut my gizzard out like that brother of Marta tried to do, and now we have no chayote vine to save me. It's all perfectly marvelous, Petra. You have a great head on your shoulders."

"You need have no fear, señor. Her husband is in prison."

"Whatever for?"

"For killing a man out of jealousy over Magdalena."

"I can only hope he's in for life."

Magdalena did not reappear after Petra left. It was a balmy night, and I sat on the steps smoking, trying to think of my work next day, but the strange, beautiful woman under my roof drew my thoughts like a magnet. I tried to think only of redheaded Castanets. I tried to think of other delectable girls. But the mysterious stranger had me in her toils. I knocked my pipe out against the bricks and tapped on her door.

She opened, a troubled, questioning look on her face.

"The evening is long," I said. "I am lonely. Won't you join me in a drink?"

She hesitated and looked down at her shining black dressing gown and pulled it closer with a modesty that successfully carved her hip into bold relief. "I was going to retire, but I'm afraid I won't sleep. I don't know whether I'll ever sleep again."

"Then I'll fix the drinks. A highball?"

"Cognac if you have it."

She came to the front room presently and tucked herself, still in her dressing gown showing the lace of her nightgown, into an easy chair.

"Cigarette?"

"Please."

I lit it for her. She avoided my eyes. We did not speak. The country night was very still. The curtain of tall trees beyond the corral was very black. She looked at the tip of her cigarette with a little frown, then gazed at me frankly, half-smiling. "You are mystified, of course. I'm plain desperate or I wouldn't be here."

"So I gathered. Petra told me a few things."

"It's not fair to you my coming here this way. I should have explained. But I was in a daze. I was going to speak tomorrow, but I had better explain everything now. Then, if you think best, I can get dressed and leave at once."

"Where would you go?"

"God knows."

"I could fix you up for a few nights elsewhere if you would prefer it that way. But I have discovered that if you are a writer, even if your life is as pure as the driven snow, people insist on providing you with scandalous behavior. I'm not worried about that, though perhaps you should be. I'm worried only about myself. It puts a strain on me, seeing you there so charming and beautiful."

She told me how she was married to Colonel Jorge Manzanares. He had only one grave fault, he was insanely jealous, she could not even speak to another man in a social gathering without his raging at her endlessly.

"That is easy to understand. He's public enemy Number One for having monopolized you in the first place."

Thoughtfully she looked at me with her big wide eyes and things happened inside me. The main trouble, she went on, was her friend Bartoldo, whom she had known since childhood. He was a tennis champ and loved other sports. For a time he and the colonel became good friends and played handball together, then the colonel began accusing her of having improper relations with him.

"It was absurd. Bartoldo has been almost part of our family since I was a little girl. We were always fond of each other, but there was nothing between us, not ever." Nothing would shake this insane fixation from the colonel's mind. He insulted Bartoldo openly, but the latter took it rather than be provoked into a fight. Her husband finally ordered her never to speak to Bartoldo again.

Months later she ran into him at the country club. She

could not cut him dead. He invited her to have a drink. Reluctantly she did so. Someone told her husband, and he threw her and the little girl out of the house without a cent. She did not know where to turn. Her parents were dead. She had a poor aunt in Tampico but no money for fare. She lived with this friend and that, hoping the colonel would relent. Instead, he spread terrible stories about her, and people drew their skirts back.

In her darkest moment Bartoldo loaned her money. Then he lost his job and could not help her, but he persuaded his landlady at his boardinghouse to take her in until he or she found work.

"There wasn't anything between us," Magdalena insisted again. "I swear it by the Holy Virgin. Bartoldo was like a father and a brother. When my little girl got sick, he sat up with her all one night."

She ran into the colonel on the street. There was a haggard gleam in his face; he asked her to come back. But his jealous fits returned. He even struck her. "Then he got it into his head my little girl was not his, and he struck her so badly he left a scar on her forehead. I comb her hair so it won't show. I went back to the boardinghouse. This time I was able to take my clothes and my jewelry, a few things to help out for a time. All are gone now."

Her eyes filled. "One day my husband stormed into the boardinghouse and killed Bartoldo, who was sick. He shot him in his bed in cold blood. Likely he would have killed me, too, had I been home."

There was a scandalous trial. His attorneys tried to prove she had been carrying on with Bartoldo but could not succeed. He was given ten years.

"He's in prison now, and my friend Bartoldo, the finest

man alive, is dead, and my life is in ruins. After the trial, his own mother, convinced I was not to blame, asked me to come live with her. I have managed alone for about six months. I worked as a servant till the husband began bothering me. When I came to Petra's last night I was at the end of my rope. I am using my maiden name so few people connect me with the tragedy, but I shall leave here—tonight if you think best."

I looked at her in her misery, so beautiful, and whether she had told her story straight, I didn't know. It didn't matter much.

"There's one thing more—the colonel has sworn he will kill me. He is half-mad now, you know."

"But since he is locked up . . ."

"He's a slippery devil and can be charming. Three weeks ago he managed to get out of prison. He returned voluntarily the same night, said he had gone to see his mother because she was sick. Bribery. Cunning. But if he did it once he might succeed again."

"It's a remote worry. I told Petra her friend could stay here, and she's one person I won't welch on."

She put her glass down, and her arms fell limply to her sides. With great dignity she said, "I'm not a child. You've been very good. I'll understand if . . ."

I broke in hurriedly, sweating a bit, "Tomorrow we shall talk some more."

And so it was I had a *femme célèbre* under my roof.

I had to rush out early next morning. When I came back in the afternoon, Magdalena was sitting in my study in a loose house dress that made her look sultry, sewing my curtains. On the table was a vase of flowers.

"There are not many flowers in the garden now," she said.

"You should give Petra money to buy some at the market."

I was out again early next day and recalled as I was returning home about five that I had not told Petra to buy flowers. I swung over to the market. Most flower stalls were closed, but I found a broad-faced Indian woman from whom I had never bought. "How much are your gladiolas?"

"A peso, señor."

I threw up my hands. "But, Niña!"

Niña—baby—is conventionally used for any woman from the cradle up to ninety. On remote highways travelers always say to a woman they meet, "*Buenos días,* Niña." Or, "May God go with you, Niña."

But the buxom Baby in the flower stand said emphatically, "It rained hard yesterday, so the price is up today, and these are beautiful."

"But it is late, and tomorrow they will not be beautiful."

"That is the price, señor, and I'm selling less than I did earlier."

Our bargaining went on good-naturedly. "I guess I'll have to let them go," I said. "Today I'm very poor."

"Folk like you are never poor."

"Today it happens to be true."

"In that case, señor, you may have the flowers for nothing." She shoved the bunch into my hands and would not take a cent.

"Tomorrow or next day I'll pay you." She was clever, knowing she would get her original price.

But she said, "Would there be any pleasure in my helping you out today if you are merely going to pay me back later on?"

"Niña, you have a heart of gold."

"Is it not better the world be happy and full of friends?"

Magdalena's eyes shone at the sight of the flowers. She arranged them with loving care.

Several times as the days slid by Magdalena said she was leaving.

"What are your plans? Where will you go?"

She had no plans, no place to go. She had not secured work.

"Maybe I can get you a government post."

She was excited. "That would be wonderful, except there are few things that I know how to do."

"That's a perfect qualification for a government post."

I took her to the movies several times and one night said, "I've just had a windfall. We'll go to the Regis to dine and dance."

"That might not be wise. It would get back to my husband." But she finally consented.

She was stunning in a black evening dress and was a marvelous dancer. Friends of hers came over to speak to us and eyed me curiously. Any one of them would have taken her off my hands at the drop of the hat. I could understand the wild colonel better.

She kept saying she wanted to go to Tampico. Her aunt was using her furniture and was giving up the house. Magdalena wanted to ship her things back to Mexico City. "I have many friends there. I'll be all right."

I made a deal with her. "I'm going on a horseback trip shortly. You've made everything nice around the house. I'll pay you back salary as my housekeeper, and that will cover your fare."

"You're trying to be nice. I don't want your money."

A few nights later we had another bad earthquake. Again I hit for the patio trailing my flag of glory, my blanket.

Magdalena rushed out with her little girl and fell into my arms. She was trembling violently, and the soft sensation was more tremendous than the earthquake.

I woke with the footsteps of gray dawn creeping into my room. It seemed as if I smelled Magdalena's perfume on my pillow, but my bed was empty. It seemed I heard the swish of soft garments and feet soft as the gray feet of the dawn. I slept again.

At breakfast I asked Lupe, "Did you scream or pray?"

"Plague it all, I didn't even wake up. None of us did."

I put Magdalena and her little girl on the train for Tampico and kissed her good-by. She clung to me and cried.

"You will be back," I told her.

"Who knows what life holds? I might come back to you, if you wanted me a little."

"Who could help wanting you, Magdalena? But I'm a bird of passage."

The next morning I took the bus for the south to start on my horseback trip. I stopped off at Cuernavaca for a few days to visit friends. I was seated on the hotel terrace at breakfast reading the *Excelsior* of Mexico.

"Colonel Manzanares, condemned for murder, escaped from prison for the second time. He has made many threats against his wife, and the authorities were alarmed. They were unable to ascertain her whereabouts. He did not show up at his mother's house this time, where police watchers were posted. He was free for two days but, as before, voluntarily returned to prison."

Though it was only ten in the morning, I ordered a double cognac.

IX

GOLDEN ACAPULCO

"EVEN the parrots are getting too civilized in Acapulco."

The barefoot shoe shiner snapped his rag smartly and told me about Don Virgilio, the schoolteacher who kept a parrot named "Esperanza" after his dead sweetheart. Whenever Mario left the classroom and the children cut up, the bird would scream *"Atención! Atención!"* But one day the parrot took French leave, and Virgilio pined so badly that his friends made him take a trip.

He mulebacked to a mountain village to visit relatives. From the steaming jungle rose a vast school of wild parrots. All in unison they screamed at him, *"Atención! Atención!"*

111

I looked up Don Virgilio in his modern schoolhouse of glass and gleaming tiles and carried him off to have drinks on the terrace of the gaudy Flamingo Hotel, three hundred and fifty feet above the sun-drenched crashing breakers. Night fell quickly, with little twilight, the way of the tropics. Rainbow lights blazed from the shore pavilions. Rumbas and tangos yammered across the still waters.

His placid moon face drooped with melancholy. "Acapulco is getting too elegant. Two decades ago, when I started teaching here, this was only a huddle of adobe and thatched huts, only a few colonial buildings around the small plaza. We lived in peace, with only the music of our own guitars."

In the morning a lyric written in soft sunlight and flowers, Don Virgilio led me along the looping new boulevards above the sea. Scarlet bougainvillaea, crimson roses, and trumpet vines tumbled in a blazing surf over the walls. The jacaranda trees carpeted sidewalks with blue petals. The new red-gold tiled mansions with Spanish-Moorish balconies, slender columns, and ultra-modern glass commanded the far-flung ocean—the beautiful new play palaces of the new rich.

Nearly four centuries ago, as now, Acapulco had been a fabulous place. Long before Boston was settled, the high-prowed galleons of Spain put in here, great sails spread, yellow and red pennants streaming, laden with the silks and spices of the Orient. British, French, and Dutch buccaneers yipped at their heels, sometimes stormed into town, looting, burning, killing, carrying off girls and gold. Stone forts were built.

But after independence the China trade vanished, the Spanish stone-paved road to Mexico City—El Camino Real

—fell into ruin under jungle vines and rains. The port became a simmering mangy Indian village cut off from the
world.

Today, once more. a paved highway loops from the capital
over majestic mountains and valleys, across great rivers, and
through flowering tropical forests. It goes through the
paradise of Cuernavaca, through the colonial gem of a town
known as Taxco, through ovenlike Iguala of the many
orange groves, and shabby, sleepy Chilpancingo, where
shortly I was to hire horses to cross the wild reaches of the
states of Guerrero and Oaxaca.

Not merely the new highway comes here, but twelve times
a day a silver-winged passenger plane swoops in over the
high mountains. World cruises make Acapulco a port of call.
Here have been built some of the finest hotels and wealthiest
chalets in the world.

With Virgilio I visited the old stone forts, their ancient
cannon strewn among the weeds, and we walked back past
the Hamacas Hotel, where guests lolled above the sea in
hammocks lashed to coconut trees. I gathered from Virgilio,
when I asked him about the history of the port, that since
the China trade nothing much had ever happened here
except tidal waves, hurricanes, wars, and revolutionary battles—till the hurricane of modern life hit it.

"What does the word 'Acapulco' mean?"

"It's Aztec—'The Place Where the Cane Stalks Were
Swept Away.' People were living here before Moses climbed
Mount Sinai."

The most delightful hours on the beaches are early morning before the tropic sun comes burning, or at twilight
when the coconuts and palms are stenciled against the rose
sky and the late light glows in the creaming waves. The

whole harbor slides softly into liquid blackness, only bolder headlines shoulder the star-studded southern sky. Here and there lights gleam from distant mountain-jungle huts, occasionally a pillar of flame from some charcoal kiln. Under the tropic moon phosphorescence streamed along our bodies. Presently the thrum of orchestras floated out from the neon lights of shore dance halls.

At all hours the beaches are assaulted by peddlers of fresh coconuts, soft drinks, beer, cigarettes, ice cream, candies, lottery tickets, sarapes, leather and crocodile-skin goods, silver jewelry, postcards, raw-fish delicacies, newspapers, sponges, starfish, shell and red-seed necklaces, mother-of-pearl, sometimes real pearls from nearby oyster beds. Supple, barefoot zambo and Indian girls come swaying with big baskets of mangoes, oranges, and chirimoyas on their head, their necks ablaze with fiery necklaces, earrings dangling against dusky cheeks. Occasionally there is an old-style embroidered blouse, low cut and sleeveless. A few years ago, as today in neighboring villages, they would have come naked from the waist up, only a red bandanna handkerchief to cover their breasts. "Yes," I told Don Virgilio, "Acapulco is getting too civilized."

A bronzed Tarzan struck up a conversation. Don Virgilio was scarcely polite.

"He's the sort to avoid." He fished out a newspaper clipping.

"There exists on the more fashionable beaches a plague of handsome gigolos, who spend the whole day in bathing attire, red trunks one day, blue the next, flowered designs at other times. These types devote themselves to exploiting young women visiting said beaches. On the pretext of teaching them to swim or surfboard, they lure them into some secluded rocky nook and there take advantage of said inexperienced girls. It is not uncommon to see these vagabonds stick by the girl all day long, eating, drinking, and enjoying himself at her expense, until he has achieved his object, then finding another, eager for romance, who will do the same."

We strolled from the fashionable beaches to Revolcadero —the Wallow—preferred by poorer townsfolk, though the surf is rougher. Bathers lounged in homemade hammocks slung between palms and swung themselves to and fro with the aid of bamboo poles. The bathing houses here are mere strips of petate matting, wide enough to conceal the dresser from shoulder to knee. Taller girls stoop.

I saw my new friend Doña Paz Mondragón off on the Saturday-morning plane—a long-skirted Indian woman with lots of blubber on her bones. Every week she loads her wares, including a crate of live chickens, lemons, and golden mangoes, on the plane and flies to Mexico City which, until several years ago, she had never seen, to sell at the Mercedes market.

"*Dios Mío!*" she sighs, laboriously heaving her bulk into the cabin. I handed up her roll of straw matting on which she intended to sleep in the market beside her wares. Tied in the fringe of her *rebozo* are tortillas, jerked meat, and chile so she won't have to put out a cent for food or lodging. Profits pay her fare. Her capital she will reinvest in sarapes, jewelry, and handicrafts to sell to tourists, who will imagine they are getting such wares cheaper in Acapulco than in Mexico City.

Her son Alfonso totes luggage, runs errands, and shines shoes. He was the one who had told me about Don Virgilio. Her next oldest son looks after the three younger children.

Her husband, Don Rafael, takes out fishing and hunting parties and is saving money to buy a motorboat.

"It was far nicer here when we grew a little corn, a few pigs, and chickens and caught fish for ourselves," said Rafael sadly, echoing Virgilio's complaint.

He took me to fresh-water Lake Coyuca, separated from the sea by a sand bar on which is perched a restaurant and dance hall. Another day he took me to more distant Papagayo—Parrot—Lake where alligators abound. We went by car, then in a hired *cayuco* dugout propelled by an Indian boatman in a wide, hip-wound sash wielding a long double paddle, with ends flattened out like elephant ears, dipping them into the water on either side like a human sidewheeler. The two-kilometer channel was arched over with blue and gold heavens of orchids and vines, noisy with birds and parrots never taught to swear. The waters were tinged orange-red by millions of white and brown mangrove and mangle trees. Their interlaced roots provided lairs for crocodiles, snakes, panthers, wildcats, and wading birds. Each hanging branch sends down fresh roots so that a single growth may extend for an acre. The mature seeds, with sharp spurs that drive deep into the mire, wind up and are violently ejected for considerable distances.

I fished for the large curricán, which puts up a good fight, by dragging a glittering nickel-plated shoehorn with spring harpoon swiftly over the surface. I had no luck, and Rafael said sadly maybe I was not cut out to be a fisherman, a fact I already knew.

"Doubtless you were meant to be a hunter." He recited the possibilities: ducks, water crows, herons, cranes, water pigeons, quail, pheasants, panukes, *joitos,* and *chachalacas.*

"What good would it do to go back to my country and'

boast that I had shot a *chachalaca?* Nobody there ever heard of such a bird."

"That is a difficult question for me to answer." He suggested shooting deer, wildcats, and many strange smaller animals. We compromised on a deep-sea fishing trip.

"That is what I really know most about," said Rafael enthusiastically. "If you land a green-spined *agujón*"—a sort of swordfish—"that will be something." It provided a great delicacy, *seviche*, "cooked" with lemon juice and garlic, ergo eaten raw. Rafael said it was the finest dish ever concocted by man.

Sharks also find the agujón toothsome. When pursued, the swordfish leaps fifteen feet out of the water. Fishermen wait for this moment to drive home their three-pronged harpoons. "Sometimes," said Rafael, with lugubrious delight, "the excited fish drives its sword right through the side of the boat. Only last month Don Andrés got such a sword right through his 'tripes,' and it did him little good, for his wife had no money for a tombstone."

"Perhaps we can harpoon a 'necktie,'" I suggested. This is a super-sized ray fish, named for its white throat marking.

Rafael snorted disgustedly. "What good are they?"

I got up a party of six. A Mexico City doctor drove the harpoon into a colossal ray fish. It raced our boat several miles out to sea, once pulled the prow under before it gave up. We hauled it well up on the beach, a prodigious stunt, for it measured nearly twenty feet across. All six of us had our pictures taken standing on its back.

The military commandant appeared, angrily striking his riding crop against his polished boots. "Who dragged this monster up on the beach?" he roared. "Tow it out to sea again. Nobody is going to stink up *my* beach."

It is not polite to argue with a Mexican military commandant. It was dreadfully hot by now, but we tugged and
we towed.

That evening, having observed our good will, he treated
us all to champagne and hired a mariachi orchestra to entertain us. Where else in the world is virtue so handsomely
rewarded?

I had a farewell dinner with Don Virgilio at a shore
dance hall under the stars. Tiring of the yammer of rumbas
and the pinwheel hips of the dancers, we strolled along the
dark Rada watching the phosphorescence. "You had better
come with me across country," I suggested. "You will find
plenty of the primitive life you like."

He recited to me an epic poem he had written about the
Mongolian slave princess in the days of the China trade.
Captured by pirates and sold as a concubine in the Philip-
pines, she was resold in Acapulco. Dashing Miguel Sosa fell
in love with her, bought her, whisked her off to Puebla, and
gave her her freedom. She was baptized as Catherine of St.
John, and her kindness to the poor, whom she fed and
nursed and whose nakedness she often clothed with garments from her own body, made her a national legend.

She had arrived in Acapulco in a low-necked, short-sleeved
blouse richly embroidered; her red flannel skirt, or zagalejo,
was covered with glittering sequins and jewels, and she
wore green silk sandals. Her hair, braided with red ribbons,
was wound tightly around her queenly head. She continued
to dress in this fashion, and over the years her "China
Poblana" costume became the attire used in the national
fiesta dance, the *jarabe,* around the sombrero rim.

Don Virgilio's poem aroused a majestic comparison, and
his arm made a wide sweep of the port. "At night the har-

bor glitters with running fire and ten thousand spangles like the whirling 'China Poblana' costume of the fiestas, the skirt brought to Mexico by a Mongolian slave princess long ago. At night the glowing hills of Acapulco, with their golden villas, dance the lively *jarabe* about the silver sombrero of the port."

Abashed by his own exuberance, Virgilio said crossly, "Come, I shall treat you to a late snack at a little dance hall tourists never see. It is called 'Esperanza'—Hope." His mouth twisted into a grotesque grin.

X

CRAZY FOREIGNERS

EYLER wired me to meet him at Iguala, and he was waiting when I stepped off the bus into that oven of barren mountains. There was a scent of tamarind from the orchards circling the little flat-roofed town.

Eyler was in a stew. He was a person who lived by set schedules and begrudged every wasted minute, and he had not been able to line up a touring car to get on to Chilpancingo, where we would outfit up for cross country. A set schedule is not the best approach to adventure in a country not given to set schedules, or when traveling in new places where the most interesting thing, something requiring leisure and attention, might turn out to be wholly unexpected. Discovery and surprise are the essence of pleasurable travel in uncharted places. To be unhurried is to savor the essence of places and peoples. But certainly Iguala, a hot, godforsaken hole, was no place for his schedule to go haywire.

Without appetite we pushed deplorable food around our plates in a dirty Chinese restaurant and went out and lolled in the plaza, our tongues hanging out. It looked as if we were stuck here overnight, when a lean, tawny young man dashed up to us and said his touring car was leaving in half an hour. We bought back seats.

But when we showed up at the corner specified, there were no other passengers, and he sent us back to the plaza to loaf for another hour. When we showed up again, half the car engine was lying on the flagstones, and his animal-like assistant did not seem bright enough to blow a whistle let alone reassemble it.

"We'll soon take off," the chauffeur told us cheerfully.

It was four o'clock before we got under way. In some miraculous manner the engine had flown together and by some miraculous intuition the other passengers appeared at precisely the right moment.

Although the heat was so overpowering, one strapping chap wore a heavy red turtle-neck sweater. He explained at great length, though no one asked him, that he had a bad cold and was taking no chances. A sallow, flat-chested girl stared silently out the car window with a perpetual worry frown, but after half an hour, as if a button had been pressed, she started talking vivaciously and kept it up the rest of the trip without once pausing for breath. A pajama-clad Indian in a big straw sombrero carried a dollar-fifty watch on a bed of absorbent cotton in a small box and consulted it every few minutes, putting his ear down rapturously to hear it ticking as though it were a child hovering between life and death. Here was one other fellow besides Eyler passionately concerned over the passage of time. However, we soon discovered that, though he was so enamored of his shining gadget, he could not read time but cocked an eye at the sun when we asked him the hour, remarking, "Do you mean God's time or the government's time [daylight saving?"]

Eyler kept frowning at his schedule. Between ten and two we were supposed to have traveled from Iguala to Chilpancingo. From two to three we were to have had lunch and a siesta. The next hour was devoted to hiring horses. Between four and five we were to call on the governor of the state.

Instead of that we were climbing in this car over ridges past little clearings with naked babies rolling in the doorways where brown women with nude torsos and glistening highlights on their polished brown skins waved as we rushed by.

"Let the governor wait," I told Eyler. "I don't like politicians anyway."

He refused to smile.

We swung down into a wide valley of the big Balsas River where crocodiles lounged on the muddy banks getting rid of their arthritis. We crossed on the fine new steel bridge to a thatched settlement of open-air stands, smoky restaurants, blaring phonographs, and mangy dogs. It was a low, sultry place, and the mosquitoes were ravenous. But the driver suddenly remembered he had forgotten to eat lunch and proceeded to do so while his passengers waited.

He ate leisurely, throwing Eyler's schedule off worse every

minute. The other passengers took the delay for granted. The sallow girl amused herself by putting coins into the juke box. The Indian squatted in the shade, staring at his watch as though it were a sleeping beauty, apparently contented to do so for the rest of time. The man with the cold stared into the simmering sun circles, his head sunk in his sweater and tapping time to the tune of Tatanacho's "Little Drunk Girl."

Theoretically our interview with the governor was over, and we were now seeing Chilpancingo, taking notes, and writing letters. Eyler, glowering at his schedule, slashed a pencil through these items. "But we shall want to have a look at Chilpancingo," I said mildly. "As for the notes and letters, we can get on with them here."

He glared at me and made another slash. There went our pre-dinner bath, and we sure needed it. Hiring horses now became a night-lantern job. "We'll get along without any letters from the governor," Eyler decreed.

"They would come in mighty handy in the back country where people are suspicious of travelers unless they bring credentials."

But Eyler was going to struggle back to his schedule through hell and high water. Even his modifications promised to be insufficient. For the chauffeur, though he had finished his meal, merely leaned back contentedly toying with a toothpick and eying the waitress. Clearly the little mongrel frizzly-haired creature was the highlight of his whole trip. To our queries as to when he planned to resume the journey, he shrugged and said, "It will be cooler later on. Why not rest the heat out here?"

"Isn't this about the hottest spot on the whole run?"

He shrugged again and watched the waitress. He liked

food, he liked girls, he liked heat, he liked music. When the sallow girl's coins gave out, he took over and played the juke box again and again. Whenever the waitress had a free moment, he kissed her behind the juke box. He could not help observing our impatience. He shook his head with a puzzled expression touched with pity, seeming to say, "Crazy foreigners! Don't know how to enjoy life."

The other passengers seemed happy. They liked standing around, looking, talking. Traveling was not so frequent an event they wished to rush to get it over with. The heat really was abating a bit. The turtle sweater was now animatedly telling the sallow girl with murderous gestures of all the men he had killed. With artistic flourishes he slit their gizzards or popped them, then buried them in his private graveyard. The Indian was pleased to continue squatting there with his watch, which worked while he did nothing, a most suitable arrangement. The mechanics of time, the clicks of time, the mysterious making of time by hidden wheels were supremely important, but Time the essence had no meaning whatever for him. I thought of the inevitable phrase in my literary contracts in connection with the date of delivery of manuscript: "Time is of the essence."

Why were these folk so blissfully letting the *élan vital* slip through their fingers? Or were they? Why could they be so comfortable and happy without comfort? Why are we northerners, for all our modern comfort, such an uncomfortable, hurried race, ever bowing to Dictator Time? All that these folk wished, apparently, was to be able to live with the living moment, whatever its texture. All that Eyler and I knew was: "This is a hot, dirty place to stay. Maybe we'll get malaria from the damned mosquitoes." In any case, all we wanted just now was to be on the move, to get where we were going next, though we did not have the slightest assurance it would be any more comfortable or rewarding.

Our car finally climbed out of the sweltering valley to the high ridge where a delicious cool breeze—that much at least we had reasoned out correctly—fanned our faces. From here —all twilight and until long after dark we looped and glided down long slopes through majestic valleys, a mighty sweep of empire. For a long time the eastern heights were tinted with gold and silver light, changing to bronze and rose. Below, in far reaches of hills and vales, chaparral and forests lay in mysterious pools of inky blackness. It was a beautiful ride, a thrilling ride at a magnificent time of day. Perhaps our chauffeur had been right, perhaps he really had known the wisdom of doing this noble stretch at exactly the right time of day.

It was dark when we jolted over the cobblestones into Chilpancingo plaza between the massive colonial church and a candy-stick gasoline station.

"We are here!" our driver announced triumphantly, not without scorn, yet pleased that our desire to get to Chilpancingo had been fulfilled.

"At least it is cool here!"

"At this hour it is always cool, but not earlier. It's too cool." He actually shivered, though the air was a balmy caress.

We crossed quaint plaza paths lined with whitewashed stones and seashells to little Hotel Bravo, simple, spick-and-span, but lots of ants.

After a ten-o'clock dinner Eyler said no word about hunting for horses by lantern light, but tumbled into bed exhausted. Weary but resolute, I went out to the plaza under the flaming stars. The chauffeur, who had worked harder than any of us, was spruced up and promenading with two laughing girls clinging to him as though he were pure candy. In the dark, narrow streets, lined with one-story adobe houses, the pad of footsteps caused me to step quickly to the middle of the cobbled way. Each time it was a sandal-shod Indian, hurrying home after late hours. On an ancient colonial stone bridge, humped high in the middle, three girls thrummed a guitar and sang. No Hollywood staging could have been more dramatic. In doorways and windows other girls were whispering to *novios*, exchanging hand-clasps and kisses. Indians slept here, there, anywhere, curled up on the stones like anthill mounds, under sarapes and big sombreros—that pliant catlike line the Indian always falls into when in full repose.

In a high corner of town a phonograph blared from a cantina. At a small dance café Indian girls in short rayon dresses and gaudy garters sat listlessly showing their wares at tables under big trees around a tiled dance-floor patio. A long-toothed angleworm in a greasy coat played a piano, with alternate verve and lassitude. The only client was a ratty little tax collector who had enough pull or nuisance powers to rate free drinks, maybe more.

Morning came like a soft tune, fleecy clouds drifting lazily in the distant silk sky, the sun playing the stops on the giant pipe-organ mountains. Eyler was beaming. He had saved his precious schedule merely by lopping off one day of God's time. In this way we were actually in Chilpancingo hours ahead. So, after all, we went to the dilapidated state capitol to present our letter to the governor from the minister of education.

Mestizo politicians, in cream-colored suits with leather

buttons, lounged in droves in the shabby antesala. Pajama-clad peasants from the back country sat stolidly on the hard benches, as if they had been rooted in the exact spot for hours, days, decades, centuries, apparently unperturbed by the time lost—just waiting on the slow wheels of bureaucratic generosity, knowing that someday, perhaps, the carved portals of the executive office would open to them.

Being "crazy foreigners," impatient, bound by a schedule, we sent the clerk scurrying in repeatedly to press for our interview. He did so with bad grace and mounting irritation, but our insistence probably saved us hours, at the price of injustice to other long-suffering souls. And yet no one begrudged our taking precedence, everybody grinned at our good luck, their broad faces saying silently, "That's wonderful you got in so soon!"

The governor, a cynical dark little Indian, encased like a stuffed pillow in a silver-gray check suit, wore a diamond stickpin in his flaring gaudy tie, and rings glittered on his fingers. Never once did he drop his cold mask of bored indifference. The minute he found what we wanted, he dictated letters instructing all local civil and military authorities to give us every assistance, then perfunctorily waved us out. No northern executive could have been more polished, efficient, or parsimonious with his time. We left slightly disgruntled precisely because he had lived up to the best traditions of our own land.

We inquired about horses. A plaza bootblack in a salmon shirt took us to the home of a plow maker. A half-wit drunk sprawled at the door. An anteater and razorback pigs were sniffing and grunting in the house and back yard. The horses, which the head of the household showed us, were half-starved little nags but he assured us they were sturdy, fast travelers. We told him we wanted to leave next morning at daybreak, and he swore by "the bigotes of an Englishman," and by his own stringy six-hair mustache, which he stroked with a great air, his belly shaking with laughter, that he would be at the hotel on the dot.

To our vast astonishment he did show up at dawn instead of midday. It was so incredible in this mañana land that we set out in high spirits. Eyler was beaming jubilantly, his schedule, minus one day, was hitting on all cylinders again.

We wound over great ridges in the rocky dry state of Guerrero, an enormous wilderness sparsely sprinkled with far-flung villages. We fell in with a train of muleteers in red sashes and jogged along in clouds of dust through growing heat, then cut across a high, barren trail along a stone ridge above the town of Tixtla. Fiesta rockets were exploding above the red-tiled roofs.

The inn, with its cool tiles and shady orchard, was a pleasant refuge, run by a buxom young widow, Enedina, who made us feel as though we were old, affectionate friends, not just chance travelers. Handsome, full of fire and fun, she was amused when we said we wanted lunch early so as to get on to the next town. Why should two intelligent people go riding around in terrific midday heat merely to see novel sights? Were there not enough cool hours in the day without making ourselves miserable? And why miss Tixtla's fiesta? The big day was tomorrow. Where would we find anything better?

"All those places you're hankering to see will still be there just as they have been for four hundred years. This neck of the woods hasn't changed in centuries, so you aren't going to miss anything however much you dally. If you take time to enjoy things, you have sweet memories." She arched and gave me a coquettish wink. "If you have no memories, it is the same as not having seen anything at all."

"We have heard that fine fiesta masks are made here."

"Tixtla used to have a famous mask maker, but he has moved away. All the folk have masks, but they treasure them for the fiesta dances. When the day has cooled off, I will take you to a woman who has extra ones."

We urged her, since Eyler's schedule demanded that we leave here right after lunch, that she take us there at once, but she refused to stir in the sun. "Not even for a new silk petticoat would I traipse across town at this hour." But she finally shrugged her ample breast, got out a pert sunshade from a carved chest, and set out, good-naturedly grumbling she would never do it except that we were "crazy foreigners." I said she was charming.

She took my arm intimately and her long lashes brushed her cheeks. "Since we like each other, promise me you'll stay until tomorrow. The fiesta in Tixtla comes only once a year. These are Tixtla's great days, costume dancing, a soccer game, a bullfight, fireworks. We'll be very, very nice to you," she added with a teasing, warm smile.

After a long trek to the other side of town, we found that the Indian woman was away for the day in another village. "So you see," Enedina told us gaily, "if you want masks you'll have to wait over until tomorrow."

She made the daughter, a shy pigtail of fifteen, open a chest and show us two fierce tiger masks lying among bright-colored fiesta costumes. "Why don't you sell them to the gentlemen?" she asked. "Your mother can always get more masks. How much?"

The girl dug her toes into a crack and twisted her *rebozo*.

"If you say so, Enedina, I'm sure Mother won't scold me."

"What will you pay?" Enedina asked us.

We suggested two pesos each.

"You are honest people," the girl said, "and if you and Enedina say the price is right, you can have them."

"That is a good price and you know it, little coyote face," Enedina told her.

Happy that her mission had been successful, Enedina was even more jaunty going back, twirling her fine sunshade, swinging her hips, and humming an amorous tune with the sheer joy of life. She had a brisk, gay greeting for everybody. Presently a rider in a spangled charro costume and a saddle encrusted with silver came along the sidewalk trying to keep in the shade. Enedina put her hands on her hips and blocked his path.

"Mr. Mayor, if anybody else rode on the sidewalk that way, you would put him in jail."

Chivalrously he swept his big sombrero to his knees, saying he wished Enedina would lock him up forthwith. With a prancing show of fine horsemanship, his silver bridle jingling, he wheeled out of our path.

"You must have many admirers," I told Enedina.

She shrugged. "Every *macho* makes eyes at me. But all they want is to get hold of my property and enjoy free meals."

"Is that *all* they want?"

She gurgled hilariously. "Oh, but the vagabonds would then lie in the hammock all day while I work. With my little property, I make a better living than most, and I prefer to be fancy free." She squeezed my arm.

She sank gracefully into an easy rocking chair on the roofed-over terrace, fanning herself. "*Madre mío,* what a walk! For no one else on this earth would I have gone."

Undoing the top buttons of her tight dress, she wiped the perspiration off her large, firm breasts without the slightest embarrassment, indeed almost with the air of wishing all who desired to enjoy the sight of her plump, perfect wares. Coolness oozed up from the red tiles, worn and old but waxed shiny, and the breeze moved in gently from the cool gardens and flowering trees. It was pleasant to watch the match-thin old servant peeling potatoes in the polished brown bowl between her calico knees. It was nice to watch Enedina, and nicer still to discover that she would exchange greedy kisses in the dark arched passageway to the dining room. She changed into fluffy organdie, and it was a joy to watch her lolling plumply in the low hammock, swinging it gently with one trim leg over the side.

Repeatedly, with mischievous eyes and a flirtatious promise, she tried to break down our determination to go on. "Stay on, you'll *never* regret it, that I promise you." The ride to Chilapa would be hot and long and dusty. The day was growing hotter by the minute, a real scorcher. "And does my inn lack proper inducements?" She moved her leg against mine and squeezed my hand under the table.

But Eyler's honor depended on keeping to his schedule, no matter how interesting the Tixtla fiesta might turn out to be. Our real goal, he reminded me, was the Mixtec Indian country. Surveying luscious Enedina, I did not give a hoot about the Mixtecans at that moment. But there was no use working at cross-purposes this early in our trip. I knew that before long Eyler's schedule would get smashed, that he would learn it could not be kept, that he, too, would relax and want to enjoy things enroute. A traveler with a fixed schedule is a traveler with a set yardstick. He might as well stay home, he is merely taking his own little world along with him, all his own rigid customs and prejudices, so that everything he sees, if he sees it, is lacking and evil.

Eyler, I could tell, was already disgusted by Enedina's casual, lazy display of her breast, a freedom unknown in the world he knew. She was a fine earthy madonna, like those of the Renaissance painters, richly sweet and beautiful. And so the two "crazy foreigners" set out in the blistering sun, not even waiting for lunch to settle in their stomachs. Enedina waved us a derisive good-by and went back to her comfortable, cool hammock. The dust rose about us in clouds.

The endless trip to Chilapa was worse than Enedina's direst warnings. The sun was merciless, each mile grimmer. Neither of us had been in the saddle for several years, and our blistered buttocks and sore muscles made every step a torture.

As the great golden ball of the sun floated in and out of the trees on western hills, we reached a rocky ravine and followed a huge water conduit, that undoubtedly fed Chilapa. Encouraged, we urged our horses to fresh effort. But Chilapa proved elusive. We wound down the narrow, hot canyon for hours and even when we emerged into a wide, fertile valley, the distant church towers kept receding like a mirage beyond endless cactus lanes, corn and cane fields, orchards and banana groves.

At a small bridge the tolltaker said, "You ride fast," and shook his head disapprovingly at our lathered horses and watched us wheel up a clay bank to follow the river with narrowed eyes that seemed to say, "Crazy foreigners."

Peasants and their women and children were coming home from distant corn milpas, tired but happy at their release from hot toil. Weeping mourners, the women wearing black tapalos and the men with black armbands on their white pajama suits, carried a dead man in a curtained litter to some distant graveyard. We climbed a small bluff into town just as the cathedral bells were tolling. Twilight was dim and cool under luxurious foliage. Walls blazed with flowers, the air was balmy and sweet. The flat-roofed place, with its oxen and asses, had a biblical flavor.

Drunk with weariness, we swung off our horses, groaning, before the Central Hotel, an annex of a large merchandise store run by a loud-mouthed Prussian who bellowed at clerks and customers alike. With an ugly snarl he led us along a patio corridor to a huge, high-ceilinged room which he informed us arrogantly was the prize of his establishment.

It was filthy, littered with refuse, the tiles grimy, the two big brass beds, with greasy linen, unmade. The fiber mats beside them were shockingly dirty. We insisted on clean linen. He glared and bellowed for the Indian chambermaid. She was just coming out of a bath, and her wet hair hung down her back.

"What can you do with such worthless creatures?" he roared. "They take a bath and leave the rooms filthy. I can't keep after them every minute. I have to be in the store. What can I do?" His bellow ended in a pitiful squeak, and he regarded us haggardly with self-pity.

The girl laughed insolently at his red face and provoked him to apoplectic abuse. She laughed still more, and he went off, mopping his brow, shaking his head, defeated. Clearly he was a stern, lost-schedule man decaying under the hot Chilapa sun. Even with the whole Wehrmacht at his command, he could never have won out against age-old ways. The only Hitler in Chilapa was the all-powerful sun.

Once his establishment had been stately, but now was merely ghastly with its gaudy red-orange wallpaper badly peeling, its enormous grimy drapes and lace curtains, its big framed gilt mirrors and pictures vainly trying to fill up the baronial expanse. One showed Christ of the Sacred Heart alongside a velvet-gowned lady with a big bustle who had just stabbed a gent in a lace collar and, with elegant indifference, was watching the blood run down his lace sleeve as he clutched his spurting wound. On the other side of the sacred picture was a nude with flaming red hair, luscious pink breasts, and rosebud teats, floating behind green gauze. Still another gilt monstrosity housed naked harem beauties herded by black eunuchs. The brash collection was completed by an aspirin calendar with a nude posing with her hands laced behind her head. Except for the lonely Christ, this was a barroom of the gay nineties.

Cold showers revived us, but we could swallow only a few mouthfuls of the Prussian's vile food and talked regretfully of Enedina's tasty cooking. We flung ourselves wearily on our beds without undressing, every muscle squealing in agony. But we had kept to our schedule, lashing and spurring ourselves and our bony nags to supreme effort. And now we were too weary to take three steps to look over this quaint, attractive town. Our schedule demanded that we push on again at daybreak.

For all the hard lumps under the soiled pink coverlet, the bed felt like swansdown. Even the sharp angle of my neck on the hard, high bolster seemed unadulterated bliss. An insistent tap on the barred windows that opened upon the narrow cobbled street brought me out of my drowsiness. I got up groaning, clutching my kidneys.

An Indian woman in dust-dragging skirts beamed unctu-

ously and motioned to two pretty girls, not more than thirteen or fourteen, standing in the shadows. They came to the
window smirking and mincing, pulling their dresses tight to
show their figures. "Which do you prefer?" asked the old
crone. She peered into the room. "There are two of you. Why
don't you take them both in and have a good time?"

This was nowhere on Eyler's schedule, and I told them to
begone.

"Or if the Señor wishes to go elsewhere by himself . . ."

"Get along with you."

"Only two pesos each, señor, and they are jolly good fun.
They will do whatever you wish." The girls giggled and
made eyes. "Or, if you like the two of them, it would be
fifty cents less," she amended.

I threatened to close the shutters in her face, though the
room was still an oven. The woman kept calling to me,
rapped several times more, then they went away. Eyler was
snoring like a mountain lion, and I sneaked a look at his
schedule on the stand beside his bed.

Thursday.
5:30. Arrive at Chilapa. (We'd arrived several hours later.)
5:30-7:30. Rest. (We'd missed out on that.)
7:30-8:00. Bathe and dress.
8:00-8:45. Dinner.
8:45-9:15. Sit in the plaza.
9:15-10:30. Make notes, read.

At this moment we should be making notes about the muleteers, Enedina's cool inn, the fiesta masks, tolltakers, country funerals. It struck me as ridiculous to have battered ourselves into insensibility just to keep his damned schedule, to

have foregone the company of sweet Enedina, to have arrived here unable to appreciate what we had found. Whatever the cost to my blistered behind, the least I could do was to see the big plaza at night. My will to do this at such an exhausted moment was as silly as Eyler's rigid schedule. I gave my hair a lick and plodded forth groaning.

The big plaza under gigantic trees was crowded. It had only one high arc light, but smoky fires burned eerily under the terra-cotta pots of outdoor kitchens. At an oilcloth covered table alongside the grass I had a beer and felt better. Another beer made me feel still better. The woman was stirring a red-brick stew in a huge olla. It could be no worse than the Prussian's stinking food which I had not eaten. "I'll try some."

She ladled out a generous portion into a green-glazed bowl, flung down a stack of fresh hot tortillas, and poured me another beer. The food was excellent, even though it scorched my throat, and the beer brought out the flame all the way down. I asked her husband, who squatted beside the olla, arms akimbo, about Chilapa, the churches, fiestas. "Where can I buy masks?"

Fiesta masks were triple underlined on Eyler's list, and with bitter laughter I told myself we would certainly buy them even if we had no time to look at the fiestas in which they were used. The woman called to a neighbor in Aztec. The latter inquired of someone else. The soft, musical tongue echoed across the plaza and back: "The Señor wishes to buy fiesta masks . . . fiesta masks . . . fiesta masks . . ."

A long-skirted crone, with a crafty face vaguely familiar, told me her niece had masks. "Very nice ones. I'll take you to see her."

Tiredness had crept back into my bones. "Tomorrow."

"It's only a wee step, señor."

At a hurried trot, her bare feet scarcely visible under her multiple skirts, she swished across the plaza and down a dark side street to an enormous double door.

Except for a faint light gleaming under a crack at the far end, it was pitch black inside, some sort of warehouse. I caught the clearly defined odor of human bodies, the sweaty stench from coffee, brown sugar, corn, leather, and harness. Presently I could make out mountains of sacks and matting bales, crates of slit bamboo lashed with rawhide. At my feet a dozen Indians were curled up in sarapes.

We stepped over their bodies. The door in the rear swung open on leather hinges. Before the faint glow of a red float lamp under a Virgin sat a paper-thin woman, her blue *rebozo* tight around her bony face and black hair. She did not turn as we entered, not a flicker of her eyes, as though she had been sitting there still as death through all eternity, staring into the dark wall, into never-ending night, yet undoubtedly aware of the red float lamp and the Virgin and the patterns made by the red glow on the Virgin's golden robe and on her own bare forearm, just endlessly sitting like an Aztec idol, paying us no attention, not even turning her head.

The old crone spoke in Aztec. Slowly the woman's opaque dead eyes turned to me, not curious, not friendly, not hostile, just passive with everlasting sorrow, like sockets of stone, like the agate eyes of a statue. It was monstrous they even moved at all. The two women mumbled in Aztec with a hint of indecent laughter.

"She says she will show you the masks," said the old crone, sniggering.

For a few minutes longer the bony woman sat motionless before the lamp, as if saying "What a nuisance!" then reluctantly, a movement far heavier than her fragile body, she lit a candle and motioned me through another door into the dark, but saying nothing.

The old crone, as we went out, gave two mysterious knocks on the partition of the next room. A quirk of fear darted through me, though nothing unpleasant could likely happen to me since the plaza folk had known where I was going. But I was among total strangers in a dark, eerie world. The queer sniggers of the old crone became sinister.

I followed the thin woman out the door into the dark, her outline barely distinguishable in the faint candlelight. She flickered on ahead of me to a small shed. There she pulled out some fiesta masks from dirty rags. I turned them over in the faint light, then jumped. The old crone was at my elbow, though I had not heard a sound. Both women watched me intently, almost breathlessly, yet oddly indifferent, too.

"They don't interest me," I said. "They aren't very good. I'm sorry I bothered you."

"You can have them cheap," said the crone.

But already the thin woman was wrapping them up in the rags again.

"You can have them cheap," said the old crone again.

The thin woman spoke sharply, with surprising energy. "Masks are something you like or you don't like. It is not a question of price, Grandmother."

Yet as she turned she measured me, tensely I felt, and it made me uneasy. Their manner told me something was afoot and that it concerned me.

With considerable relief I stepped back into the room with the red float lamp. Light now flickered in through reed matting that screened off the adjacent room. The crone spoke in Aztec, and a girl's voice answered, laughing.

"I shall show you the best mask you ever saw," said the old crone, sniggering. "This one you will want." She lifted a burlap curtain for me to pass ahead and let it fall on my heels, not accompanying me.

Before me stood one of the little girls previously offered me at the hotel window. Except for her red slippers, the flower in her hair, and her long, flashing earrings, she was stark naked and smiling invitingly. Her hands were laced behind her straight black hair and her neat belly was thrust forward—the exact pose of the girl on the aspirin calendar. It was so patently copied, I had to laugh. In the candlelight her sleek brown body had a golden aura and was polished with glistening highlights. Her breasts had sprouted nicely but were still girlish. She was slim and round, her body devoid of hair like all native women. She waited smiling, flickering her long eyelashes, then rolled her hips.

Angrily pushing aside the two conniving women, who were peeping through a crack, I stumbled out through the dark warehouse. In spite of my care, I stepped on the outstretched hand of one of the sleepers at the outer door. He grumbled and rolled over. In the street I licked the coolness of the night. Holding my sore back, I plodded to the hotel.

Eyler was still snoring, his mouth open, bathed in sweat, still in his clothes. He had not stirred since I had left. I tiptoed to his bedside and picked up his schedule. It said nothing about girls, naked or otherwise. I scribbled.

9:30-11. Masks unmasked. Nude calendar girl.

XI

MOUNTAIN SHUTTLE

THE sun was pouring liquid gold through the window bars when my gummed eyes came open. According to our schedule, we should be high among the mountain pines to the west, but it was now a frazzled eight-thirty of another scorching day. I hung my legs over the side of the bed. My back squealed like an orchestra tuning up, and I sat dazedly smoking a cigarette, trying to gather energy to get to the shower stall.

Eyler jerked out of a sound sleep. "We're late!" he cried. In midair he caught hold of his kidneys and fell back. He held one foot and sock uplifted with a grimace of pain. On his second try he noticed my notation on his schedule. His jaw dropped. He puzzled over it for a long time, but said nothing.

We fought for breakfast against flies and mangy curs. Eyler's face looked as if he had found his Christmas stocking empty. "We're certainly wasting time." He rose decisively, but grabbed his kidneys again.

I suggested we sit in the plaza shade till we got some oil in our joints. Our schedule was blasted again. Maybe the "crazy foreigners" could settle down to have a real look at things—a whole day late, I thought bitterly, thinking of Enedina's soft mouth.

The air was sweet and caressing. Eyler did not mention his schedule again, but soon began thinking up duties. "We ought to present our credentials to the mayor," a courtesy expected of strangers in small Mexican towns.

"The mayor won't throw any fit about it."

But to the mayor, like soldiers, we marched. He was a lame man in a red shirt and black glasses and got rid of us coldly like third-class circulars consigned to the wastepaper basket.

Eyler's next chore was to parcel post our masks and other handicrafts to lighten our travel load. We got paper and twine from the Prussian. "Junk!" he bellowed disgustedly.

The postmaster had us declare the contents. "Fiesta masks! What a foolish thing to waste postage on! The Indians are children!" He was Indian himself.

"To get masks is the only reason we journeyed to Guerrero," I told him severely. His lips pursed to words he did not utter. "Crazy foreigners."

Determined to find activity, Eyler decided we should get fresh mounts and start out this same afternoon. But we

lounged in the plaza and merely thought about horses. Even
to talk required ginger. We soon had to. Curious townsfolk
struck up conversations. I asked if Chilapa had received
land under the new agrarian law.

"This is a religious center," said a man in a tan suit and
too-small hat. Chilapa had been a bishopric before falling on
evil days. "Even if the government were to give us lands,
we will never accept stolen goods."

Argument swirled about. "And who stole the lands long
ago?" demanded a thin chap in a striped green shirt. "Who
are you to say our people shall not eat and be free?"

Passions rose, but in typical Mexican way the more bitter
the arguments, the more courteous the disputants became,
perhaps realizing that keyed-up feelings might bring vio-
lence.

We downed some lunch, but when we started to look for
horses, the ovenlike air drove us to our cooler tiled room. We
did not stir until four o'clock.

"We're as bad as the natives with our long siesta," I told
Eyler severely.

"Maybe it did us good," he admitted grudgingly. "But we
have to find horses today."

"I have to have some iced beer before I'll stir one step."

But the iceman hadn't come yet. Anyway, people
squeaked in horror, iced beer will make you sick. We hunted
up the iceman ourselves. His pushcart was covered with wet
newspapers.

"*Buenos días, amigo*. We wish ice for some beer."

"But, señores, I never sell less than four centavo's worth."

This proved to be a chunk of about three cubic feet. We
took turns lugging it to the hotel. The beer vitalized us back
to horses.

The owner agreed to show up at daybreak next morning and actually did show up at six-thirty. "We've lost a whole day in Chilapa," grieved Eyler as we spurred off.

"Anyway, we saw some of it."

"We could have seen plenty in half an hour," he snorted.

I mulled over this, thinking of the slow, quiet wheel of the day, the changing shadows on the tinted buildings, the rhythm and shuttle of life. I recalled the jolly servant girl, emerging glistening from the shower room, buttoning her tunic over one shoulder and mocking at the bellowing Prussian. I recalled the twilight funeral, the candlelights in the cathedral, folk kneeling with rapt faces, the tinkle of the bell in the Mass. I remembered the starlit night in the plaza of eerie charcoal fires when Eyler had been snoring on the dirty pink bedspread. Once more I saw that woman motionless as an Aztec idol before the red lamp, the vicious little prostitutes, the peasants sleeping in a warehouse doorway, about the children in the little adobe schoolhouse whose shrill parrot voices recited in unison, oriental style. What would they grow up to be after parroting words about the Mexican government, the constitution, and the flag? Would they be two-peso whores in front of hotel windows showing their bodies? Would they be weavers of mats and straw hats? Would they be making those woven sandals that whisk over the stones of this great land? Would they march off to war? To a new revolution?

A century earlier out of that lowly peasant stock in nearby Tixtla—Enedina's town—had emerged as one of Mexico's greatest leaders and presidents the man who had abolished slavery and for whom this state was now named. Which of the little tousleheads would rise to similar eminence? Or none?

No, a lifetime in little Chilapa would never give one all its secrets, past, present, and future—all its hopes and sorrows and laughter. A painter would know he had to live with the changing light on old walls a long time before daring to put it on his canvas.

Our way lay across wilder mountain country. By midafternoon we reached Petitlán, beside a green-banked river among thriving cornfields. Following under the crest of a majestic wooded ridge, we plodded into Atlixtac—White Water—at nightfall and put up at the neat dirt-floored *mesón*, smelling of fresh blue calcimine. Gone was the heat, and we shivered in the thin air off the waterfalls, but we had kept to our schedule and Eyler was proud of us.

Schoolteacher "Professor" Manuel Doblado showed us over the town, hopping along eagerly with his crutch and one leg. A former telegraph operator, he had paid the price of revolution and freedom. His school was clean as a whistle, and the fine garden was neatly enclosed in a bamboo fence to keep out village pigs. To amuse us, he organized a volleyball game in which he took part. With the amazing agility of some cripples, he could vault clear across the court with one wild crunch of his crutch.

Supper was served by the *mesón* cook. Her long braids dangling down her chest, instead of her back, coquetted with the soup, and she licked off the ends.

That night Doblado staged an elaborate impromptu school program. The hilarious bandleader wore an orange-and-red-plaid shirt and plaid sarape, and his sandalshod or barefoot players pulled out that queer modernistic dissonance beloved by native ears. Most of the girls were barefoot but wore bright rayon dresses and elaborate glittering glass combs in their tightly braided hair. Everybody worked hard to entertain us, townsfolk and children. One bovine schoolgirl danced clumsily in borrowed boots and sang *"El Amorcito Consentido"*—Pampered Little Love—a sentimental ditty that fluttered her balloon bosom and brought tears to her big black eyes. A couple did a *"Baile de Chile,"* not so hot as its name, accompanied by odd tooting music. Endless songs and recitations were rendered with set formal gestures. When we were ready to drop, the chairs were cleared away for dancing. I clasped an ample girl about the middle. Her front was soft as mush, but her ribs were bands of steel. She danced awkwardly, blushing furiously. I was scared to death I would step on her bare toes. All I could do was jiggle, then we settled down to a sort of body-to-body wiggle. She warmed up, forgot her embarrassment, and her eyes closed ecstatically.

As Eyler and I walked back through the chilly night to our cold, damp *mesón,* he remarked dourly that the party was pathetic and crude. "What these people need is a little guidance."

"Crude or not it was very beautiful and real. What do you want? A perfect, mechanized Roxy leg show? But people in a Roxy audience don't sing. They don't dance. They just sit and listen to canned music. Here these people danced and sang and made their own music. Crude or not, that was far more important for the human soul."

I shut up. It's not wise to argue after riding all day in the saddle and dancing half the night. Besides, we had a schedule to keep, and we needed all the rest we could get. Our cots at the *mesón* were made of loose bamboo rods laid across "horses" and covered with a straw petate. When we tried to sleep, the rods moved under us like a factory production belt steadily transporting our legs into space until we slipped off with a noisy thud. We spent a busy night.

But we were up at five in the predawn. Gingerly we washed our faces in the icy plaza fountain and munched some dry bread. The towering black mountains were cardboard silhouettes edged with faint silver.

The morning stayed crisp so we made good time. We lunched at a crossroads store and in late afternoon reached Tlapa—a large center remote from road or railroad, in a wide, magnificently fertile valley ringed by jagged peaks and dotted with bright little settlements among huge avocado, banana, coconut, and olive groves. White bolls puffed out from tall cotton trees. Wide, lush fields of corn and sugar cane rippled in the afternoon breeze.

Tlapa is built on three sides of a colossal colonial arcaded plaza overlooking stony river flats where a new brick schoolhouse was going up. We passed the municipal palace and stores and rode down a cobbled street past a restaurant and movie house to a hotel which we entered on horseback through a wide corridor. One wall was decorated with a former theater drop, painted with angels, golden trumpets, and palm trees framing curlicue ads of *La Barata Tienda*—The Bargain Store—and Hotel Central in Chilapa. We scoffed at the grandiose claims for that atrocious establishment. The other wall bore large mottoes:

Guests making own beds and providing own linen and blankets
    allowed twenty-five per cent reduction.
Public women strictly forbidden.
The furnishings of this hotel will not be loaned.

We wondered why anybody would want to borrow the furnishings. Our lofty beamed room, divided by flimsy canvas partition reaching halfway to the sagging ceiling, was bedecked with flyspecked murals of a lake scene. Into an oilcan, painted green with yellow blossoms, had been soldered a small brass faucet to provide water for a purple porcelain bowl on a shaky three-legged table with a yellow lace covering. A rusty pail contained faded paper flowers. Light was provided by an ancient brass lamp. Our barred windows opened on the street. Our first view was of an Indian taking a bowel movement in the gutter in front of the movie house while a band went down the street past him announcing the evening's movie: *"Reporter de Jolijud"* —Hollywood Reporter.

We paid our respects to the mayor, a sullen mestizo who obviously considered outsiders, especially foreigners, an unwanted nuisance. But everybody else in Tlapa was extremely cordial. The local druggist, a short, frayed, brown man, loaned me his manuscript history of the town. It must have cost him long research and showed considerable local patriotism.

The original name of the community, and for years after the Spaniards conquered it, had been Tlachichimoloapan, "The Place of Red Waters." Many tragedies had overtaken the place: pestilences, earthquakes, fires, wars, uprisings, revolutions. It had been razed repeatedly and each time rebuilt. Few other places in history have been battled over more than this remote town in the smiling plains of interior Guerrero: by pre-Spanish tribes, by the Spaniards, the armies of Independence, the French, and in later years by recurrent waves of revolutionists. Here, with a handful of men, Porfirio Díaz routed a whole French army, by sending Indians in small groups to every eminence to beat drums and shoot off muskets. The French, believing they were surrounded by a vast force, had crumpled up at the first charge.

The place is singularly complex, being divided into four distinct linguistic wards, Tlapanec, Mixtec, Nahuatl or Aztec, and Spanish. Newcomers from the hinterlands, in some cases not speaking any of the indigenous languages, squat in a special ward in the river bottom, back of the new schoolhouse, called "Cuba." Each ward has its own language, fiestas, trusted elders, churches, and customs, and are almost towns within a town. Spanish is fairly universal because of the well-to-do foreign merchants on the plaza and its being the official language, but most of the people speak it badly with only a smattering of words, and the more dominant tongue is Tlapaneca, which is spoken through all the vast region on south. The northern area is Nahuatl, and the southeastern sweep of mountains and valleys is Mixtecan. For centuries Tlapa has been the meeting ground, in peace or in war, of these ancient cultures and still is.

Thus the older pre-Spanish cultures, decapitated by the Conquest, have kept on vegetating like headless organisms. For three centuries Spain ruled. The plaza, central buildings, churches, the outward forms of government remind one of Spain's long influence. Some local customs also bear the impress of elements from the China trade crossing the country. Early in the nineteenth century Spanish culture was beheaded and since then, severed from its overseas roots, it has been slowly draining out into the broad sands of older native life and habits. Thus after independence, two headless cultural organisms jostled side by side. Now it is mestizo, the man of mixed blood, long the outcast go-between of both cultures, who is the dominant political ruler.

But a new shadow looms, the Colossus of the North, the United States. Even in Tlapa, people are aware of the relentless drive of the outside atomic and industrialized world, though, for the present, Tlapa is largely self-sufficient and self-centered, drowsing under its thatched and tiled roofs, not too deeply concerned. Its people eat spicy foods and play and flirt. They work, and joy in the steady cycle of their crops, some of which are harvested three times a year. In Tlapa, Eyler finally tore up his schedule once and for all. He really wanted to penetrate some of the mysteries of this hybrid community, and that could not be done on schedule.

Here we bought more fiesta masks, gay and fierce ones. Native dances here interweave with work and religion, love, life, and death. The folk dance the "Tecuanes" endlessly to flutes and tambors, a satire poverty dance in tattered clothes and palm-straw hats rising to a conical point that vibrate with every movement of thigh and shoulder. They dance the "Chichuachuas." They dance the "Apaches," feathers in their hair, faces painted, red flannel skirts swirling wide. They dance "Los Vaqueros," a cowboy dance, and "Los Locos," the "Crazy Men." By then we were no longer merely "crazy foreigners," for we had forgotten our schedule and had ceased to be in a hurry. No longer did we rush in and out of our hotel as though we had cockleburs under our tails. We sauntered. We felt the solid cobbles under our feet and the rich, teeming soil close to our nostrils. We talked leisurely to the good-natured folk in the plaza, the market, and in their homes, and the Tlapans took us to their bosoms and hid no secrets from us.

Once more we were up in the pinelands. About one o'clock, after seven hours in the saddle, we stopped in front of a village store in a tiny mountain settlement. A thunderstorm drove us inside along with a crowd of muleteers, who filled the place with their concentric circles of vast straw sombreros, a flippant, carefree breed with stark, corn-sweat odors, laughter, and sly jokes. It was a typical Indian store with a meager stock but more adequate than that of El Morenito in Coyoacán.

The owner, a brown, thin-faced woman in red bandanna and flaring ankle-length skirts, deftly weaving a straw mat every free moment, for that is the prevailing local industry, put her work aside to get lunch for us. "You are really done up," she told us. "Come inside and rest on my bed."

A bed, rather than a straw mat, was a real luxury in these parts. The inner room was cool and dim, only a few chinks of light through the thickly thatched walls, and we dozed off.

An urchin tiptoed in to get a bottle of cooking oil. His face was scaling, his eyes watery, and he was wobbling on his pins. My eyes popped wide open. "*Muchacho,* you have been sick."

"*Sí,* señor. Smallpox."

"When did you get up?"

"Yesterday."

"I suppose you slept in this bed?"

"Yes, with Mother."

We bounded off the bed as though it were crawling with ants and sat gingerly on reed stools, our flesh creepy.

Lunch was served under a thatched ramada cooled by a breeze from a wooded ravine, but our appetites were gone, and we left our hostess in near panic.

"She sure helped us maintain our schedule," I said drily.

Eyler frowned. "I wouldn't have minded resting in that bed a bit longer."

At a town farther on a federal school inspector joined us

as a companion and guide, and we continued south through arid country and towns with weird, unpronounceable names. Though only a few miles apart, often different languages were spoken—fragments of peoples shoved out of more fertile areas by stronger folk centuries before the Spaniards came.

At picturesque Zalpatlahuac—Red Sand—though some children could garble a few words of Spanish, the only spoken language was Aztec. We climbed the eighty-five stone steps to the church, a bare chapel of black-and-white tiles, with a painting on wood of an Indian bringing offerings. Several kneeling worshipers were just recovering from smallpox. We saw many cases in all stages.[1]

In Quicahuitalatzala—Slanting Rain—we found only four people able to speak Spanish, the rest spoke Mixtecan. And here a smallpox epidemic was raging, not a doctor available. The church, decorated with bright strips of paper, was crowded with frightened worshipers, praying for God to ward off the disease while they spread it by rubbing close. Ninety-three children out of a population of 440 were sick; fifty deaths already.

We hated to turn tail and run back to civilization, so we watched our personal hygiene and prayed that earlier vaccination would prove effective. Determinedly we pushed on to Atlamatalzingo del Monte, perched on a high ledge and relatively free from the epidemic. Everybody here spoke Spanish, for it had been one of the few rural places that had had a school back in the Porfirio Díaz days.

Life was difficult, for the village fields were half a day's travel away and were neither extensive nor fertile. To eke out a livelihood, everybody, from tots to grandparents, was

Since this visit smallpox has been stamped out in all Mexico.

weaving sombreros. A rapid weaver could make three hats
a day, which sold for five centavos each, leaving a profit
above the cost of the straw, which had to be brought in
from the hot country, of about thirteen centavos, the sole
income of many. The hats, we were told, were mostly
shipped to China, where even the coolies could not make
them so cheaply.

We passed by Xochapa and Talpahuán, which sell their
daughters into marriage or concubinage, and reached
Quoatzquitengo on the edge of a small, fertile valley below
heavily wooded slopes. The people were proud that their
forefathers had received a special parchment from the great
Vicente Guerrero, awarding the town the title of "Purísimo"
because they had melted down the bells, organ pipes, and
metal crowns of the Virgins and saints into cannon and bullets in the independence struggle. Not so proudly it already
boasted sixty-five smallpox deaths out of a population of
780. Most of the town was down, but school still kept.

"The children won't stay away anyway," the teacher said,
"so the ones who are going to live might as well keep on
learning."

The unfenced school gardens were being eaten up by
town animals. The building, freshly calcimined, was dangerously cracked from a recent earthquake. The walls were decorated with maps and commercial calendars of décolleté
women. There was the aspirin calendar. Shades of Boston!

A remote red trail led to a mountain spur on which stood
Mixtecapa. We eased our bones in front of the thatched
mud-walled town hall, about as big as a triple-hole out
house, and watched a ragged Indian planting corn by drill
ing holes with a stick. The poverty-stricken town has the

hospitable custom of setting aside the products of a jointly cultivated plot to be used to entertain visitors. No one who passes through Mixtecapa can pay a cent. Food, however, was scant; we were given two hard-boiled eggs, one tortilla each, and a pinch of salt. Salt in these regions is worth its weight in gold.

Paraje de la Montana, we were told, was only a short jaunt away. We climbed higher among the pines, up one gigantic ridge and down another, the ravines more precipitous each step. The air was thin and cold. The town did not appear, but a chance Indian foot traveler told us cheerily we were almost there.

We spurred ahead, expecting to see it just over the next ridge. But not a human habitation showed in all the vast wilderness. We rode for four hours more. Another Indian told us cheerily we were just arriving.

Distance means little to these tireless travelers, who jog trot over the trails all day, frequently with heavy loads, and so it was not until nightfall that we finally sighted the town on a spur far below us. It took us an hour of difficult descent in the dark to reach it.

Paraje de la Montana was a raw new settlement among fresh tree stumps. Though the climate was chill, the improvised houses were of the flimsiest thatch. The church was merely a mud dugout, the town hall a shack, and the school, if larger, had no furniture and only a dirt floor.

Not so long ago this whole region had been a great cattle and goat range, owned by a favorite of the Porfirio Díaz dictatorship. During the Zapata agrarian revolution he'd had to flee to Mexico City, where he died. When things quieted down his son came back but was killed. There were no heirs, and the property reverted to the state. Folk migrated out from Tlapanec centers to carve out new homesteads and villages, a fresh conquest of the frontier. The immemorial owners, the Indians, were retrieving their ancient patrimony, and Paraje de la Montana was the most recent of these settlements.

We met with no cordial reception. The barefoot schoolmaster evaded our questions sullenly. The mayor told us we should move on, there was little food, for it was just before harvest time. We made a house-to-house canvass and all we could buy was one egg a piece and three inches of corn in a bucket for the horses. The people were actually close to starvation, living mostly on roots.

What little food surplus there was had been used up by the visit of the Malinaltepec priest the previous day, who had ridden in with his "sister-in-law" to cook for him because he could not stand ordinary village cooking. He had "flown into a rage" because the village could provide no bed for him. A villager was posthasted fifteen miles to borrow a heavy iron bed and had trotted back with it on his back, doing the round trip in less than five hours. The priest had also talked about the "Godless state school," which accounted for the teacher's uneasiness and the dour attitude toward the school inspector who accompanied us.

The atmosphere grew so ugly that he laid down the law, telling the mayor he had to put us up in the city hall or in the schoolhouse. The señores had letters from the minister and the governor and were entitled to every hospitality. This was an illegal squatter settlement. Did the mayor wish to bring in troops and have his settlement burned?

The next day we climbed over a gigantic knife ridge,

great abysses only a few feet on either side, and down to the hot country. Here food and fruit were abundant. But the rain fell in torrents, and we lay under a thatched roof and listened to its endless patter. But mornings were clear as a song, and we wandered about enjoying the bright sun after the high mountain chill.

School was not in attendance because the roof leaked and the floor was a sea of mud. The villagers grew sullen when we asked why they did not patch up the place. They said they were "too busy" building a new curatage for "the little father," who for the moment lived in a neat cottage in a bower of roses atop the hill. He was a jolly, roly-poly fellow.

We went to the river to bathe. Village girls came down with red ollas or five-gallon oil tins for water, which they filled and carried on their heads gracefully, never spilling a drop. Presently one of the priest's servants came for water. She was a town girl in short skirts and rolled stockings. As she lay on her belly on a stone, scooping up water with a hollowed gourd, the tan skin on the back of her legs showed. She was brazenly flirtatious and with a hitch of her skirt said she'd be back at twilight in the bushes—"if we would like it." She was a counterpart of the small-town American hoydens who lurk around railroad stations for traveling salesmen.

About a week later, we climbed back through the mountains, passing gloomy Paraje de la Montana by, and worked down a mighty ravine along a trail dangerously slippery with pine needles. We crossed a big river and followed a tributary up along a narrow gorge showing only a narrow strip of apple-green sky far above us, and reached the terraced streets of Malinaltepec on a river shelf. We jumped

our horses over fallen telephone poles and drew up before
the city hall over which floated the flag of Mexico's *1910*
centenary celebration!

We found ourselves back in the smallpox zone. The place
was poor. Even the men were barefoot here. They ground
their immemorial food, corn for tortillas, on primitive stones.
Most of their cloth was home woven. Western civilization
had made few dents here.

The school, during revolutionary days used as a barracks
and still smelling of manure and lysol, is a barnlike place
with a high peaked ceiling, its beams crossing in space. A
big crucifix hung over the teacher's desk. The school inspector took the teacher to task for this, telling him it was illegal.

We visited the priest, the one who had gone to Paraje de
la Montana. He was a fine scholar and linguist, widely traveled, and would be at ease in any capital in the world, but
here he was lodged in a remote primitive village, a week's
horseback ride from the nearest railroad or highway. He
was expensively dressed, his curatage luxuriously furnished.
Through an open doorway we glimpsed his bed, heaped
four feet deep with silk and lace pillows and draped with
pale pink silk hangings. A manservant in a Palm Beach suit
and tan shoes handed us cigarettes from a monogrammed
silver case and played us classical music on an expensive
phonograph.

"Don't you miss more cultivated society?" we asked him.

"I am fond of my books and my music and my duties.
Once a year I visit my old mother in Mexico City for several
weeks, but I am always eager to get back here where there
is a little malice in men's hearts."

"You must find considerable hardship traveling through
the back country."

"It is tough, but I love it, though my stomach is delicate and chile is poison even for iron stomachs."

We joked about his making the villagers send off for a bed.

"Don't imagine it was solely for my own comfort. I have slept on straw mats, even on the cold ground many times, but I put these simple people to extra trouble purposely. It is the only way they come to realize there are better ways to live. Presently the town, rather than sending off for a bed, will buy one. Presently a few peasants will learn to like a bed more than a straw mat. It is slow, you can't force them directly to do things. That always fails. Only by example."

He told us of his efforts to raise material and spiritual standards. "Nothing much can be done until their diet is changed, and that's a terribly high wall to climb. But their corn diet keeps them hungry. There is not enough fertile land in this rocky state to grow enough corn. I have labored for years to get them to grow rye and barley and wheat. I've bought the seeds and given them out free. But they are a stubborn people when it comes to any change."

He had learned the difficult local language. Like some oriental tongues, the meaning of words depended on the pitch. "When I first came, I learned the word for 'peach,' but whenever I used it people snickered. Later I discovered that at another pitch it meant 'wildcat' and, at the pitch I was using, the most intimate part of a woman's anatomy. No wonder they snickered."

The priest and the inspector soon clashed on things educational. The priest said he was anxious to cooperate with the school, but it was immoral because it was coeducational, so he had to fight it. The inspector floundered through theories of modern education, from Pestalozzi to

Dewey, but was answered with only a condescending smile. He went out red with anger. "Now you see what we are up against. Now you see what it costs to maintain that man in luxury. What chance has our school, headed by a barefoot schoolmaster?"

"Maybe that's to the credit of the church and to the discredit of the government."

"He wants only church schools," said the inspector hotly. "The only thing we can do is run him out of here."

So was the curtain briefly lifted on the long, intolerant struggle that had drenched Mexico with blood.

In the morning we called on the mayor, a mean, hard little man, one of the few villagers who wore shoes. On his desk in the hot air lay five tubes of smallpox vaccine utterly spoiled, of course. No wonder Indians vaccinated jumped to the conclusion that the government was malevolently vaccinating them with the disease. In places this fear was so strong that federal troops had had to vaccinate the people by force.

Most people here were antagonistic to us and kept us under close surveillance. They were vastly relieved when we cleared out. Their hostility, we learned, was chiefly owing to the legend that their forefathers, when the Spaniards came, had buried a great treasure of gold and precious stones under what is now the town hall. The folk believed that outsiders came only to seek this store. Someday, when it is safe, the people intend to dig it up, then everybody in Malinaltepec will be wealthy and prosperous, a sort of New Deal. With that prospect dangling before them, they do little to improve their present lot.

We rode on through wilderness. To smallpox-ridden Concepción above a big banana grove, and past Texioyetepec, where all the villagers were putting up a new stone wall around the cemetery. Other villages rose on far red bluffs. Way below us lay the thatched roofs of Tototepec. Following a dry barranca beside a telegraph line, we reached Xalpa. We were greeted by music from a band under the colossal arcades of the town hall, just below a lofty church with a lighted cross. A fiesta was in progress, and the folk were in gala costumes. The mayor greeted us like long-lost brothers. His breath reeked of tequila, he was barefoot, and his tattered clothes not too clean. Even during the fiesta the people incessantly kept weaving straw hats. Even when they talked their brown fingers flashed deftly. They laid aside their work only to dance.

The band played continuously. Now and then the breeze snuffed out the candles under the arcades. The faint rays of light brightened the colorful costumes as the folk shuffled over the worn brick pavement and gleamed on jewelry and chains of gold coins and glass gems in high combs. Fluttering colored papers were strung overhead for decoration.

We were taken to supper in a thatched jacal. The women, cooking in a back shed, came in only to serve—tortillas smeared with red-hot chile, and atole, a sweetish gruel of chocolate and ground corn.

Our host had an infected arm from a nasty machete slash, and it was swollen two sizes. With a grimace he extended several fingers for us to shake. His skin was on fire. Herbs had been put on to draw the infection, but I doubted if he would live beyond our visit. A doctor would likely have amputated immediately. They had no penicillin, and there was no doctor closer than a week's horseback travel. He

merely shrugged when we urged him to set forth at once to
get proper medical attention.

We went back to the fiesta on the town-hall porch. Mostly
their dance and play lacked animation. The one vibrant
note was that constant flash of weaving brown fingers in the
candlelight, an endless shuttle, never pausing. That flash
and shuttle were a race against hunger.

XII

ARROWS AT THE SUN

WE were recuperating from our difficult Tlapaneca trip back in Tlapa. Eyler, though he had boiled all water and used chlorine tablets, was down with dysentery, and I, who had taken potluck with water, had had no trouble. The specific he had brought along soon brought him back, which was fortunate, for even a big place like Tlapa had no doctor, though a charlatan with an electric shock machine was curing, as he advertised, such diseases as grippe, syphilis, heartburn, malaria, and yaws. The Indians, of course, who have a great knowledge of herbs, had their *curanderos* but were apt to mix good remedies with chicken gizzards, frogs' hearts, and black magic.

161

We set out for Alcoazauca in the face of warnings by two traveling Spanish merchants that the road was infested with bandits who might kill or rob us. Soon we were in the harsh easterly Mixteca region, semi-barren and rocky until we got into the high forests. For miles we struggled down a slippery sandstone trail, crossed a wide meadow country in drenching rain, and reached our destination, unharmed, by late afternoon, riding into the plaza through swarms of squealing long-snouted pigs.

The plaza is flanked by impressive colonial buildings badly cracked from numerous earthquakes. Cool arcades shaded the large sidewalk flagstones. The town hall, with conventional bell-shaped façade and clock, was the only recent building, but it, too, was badly cracked. Such a bad earthquake had occurred while it was being constructed that the head mason was so frightened he died.

Eyler had a badly infected hand, there was no doctor, but an herb woman applied a pack of crushed nasturtium and other leaves, and in a few days the wound was clean.

The river here, the people told us, is "greedy for gold," and they told how about fifty years previously the houses on the west side of Main Street were swept away. A large chest of gold, from the house of a miser, was found clasped tightly in the roots of an uptorn tree. The river's irate conduct had been due to its lust for gold, for those who tried to reach the treasure were drowned, and it was eventually lost.

The town orchestra played constantly for us, sweet, sad music floating on the baked air of the sun-drenched plaza. Their fine instruments: mandolins, guitars, violins, and bass viols, had been made in nearby Quiquepan, with machetes for tools. The wood is dressed down with river sand and polished with vegetable oils. Metal parts are also handmade though some are imported. The instruments sold for from a peso for a mandolin to four pesos for a bass viol.

We rode upstream to Tlapacingo, a sprawling hill village. Its heavily buttressed church was also badly cracked, the tower ruined. We ate an early lunch in among long-snouted pigs in a jacal shaded by a bright red *itahuatl* tree. We climbed on up into the mountains through fragrant pines spattering drops from a recent rain. The fallen needles were like red hairs and full of white spider nests, a thick, slippery carpet. We reached a mighty ridge against the sky, the boundary between the states of Guerrero and Oaxaca, and late afternoon from an eagle-perched crag looked down on a golden speck far below—the town of Silicayoapan, the royal gateway to the Oaxaca Mixteca region. The towering white church rose from among gardens and flat roofs and colored tiles. Little puffs of white smoke broke in the sky soundlessly. Apparently some fiesta was being celebrated.

All the rest of the afternoon we wound down and down till we could hear the pop-pop-pop of the rockets. Quite late in the cool of the day we crossed a stream and climbed up among the tilted rambling lanes. We learned that the constant din of fireworks was because this was "The Holy Month of the Virgin," and it would keep up day and night for four weeks. The ungrudging adoration cost the town a pretty penny and, in relation to resources, was as heavy a drain as war on more prosperous lands.

We put up at a large *mesón* in the lower part of town. It had a patio a block square, flanked by the living quarters, corrals, stables and sheds, pens and coops. We were constantly colliding with or tripping over fowls and animals. Our room had only two canvas cots and a table bearing a candlestick, but the wooden slide window opened to a majestic panorama of green valley, crisscross cornfields, clumps of woods, and thatched huts beneath a silky sky deepening to indigo.

We ate at the plaza restaurant at an outdoor table on a brick porch, with chickens perched before our noses. Near us was the town fountain and a pool, open to dust and manure, where the townsfolk, burros, horses, pigs, goats, fowl, and birds secured water.

In the morning we visited the shops of leatherworkers, for this town provides the saddles for a great inland empire extending across three states. A simple uncarved wooden-leather contraption costs as little as five pesos. Those made to order, with fine tooling and hammered silver, may cost thousands of pesos. The leather is prepared in big red tanning vats. Leather-aproned workers were scraping hides and pounding the leather to pliability, others were cutting out designs or sewing seams, some by hand, some with machines.

From a storekeeper we bought several white sandstone Mixtec idols unlike any I had ever seen in any museum. I also found a big grinning hermaphrodite idol in rough brown sandstone which I later gave to Diego Rivera.

In the evening the town secretary called on us. We sat in the balmy moonlight of the patio. He spoke bitterly of the armed depredations of the Cristeros, religious fanatics, and told of the new lands for the peasants, the school, his hopes for a new, strong, prosperous Mexico.

We had to get fresh horses. The only ones available were a fine plump sorrel and a scrawny little black mare with accordion ribs. We matched coins, and the sawbones black fell to me. We left at four o'clock in pitch-black darkness and risked our necks galloping blind though the Barrio de

Carmen and along a maguey lane that dipped in and out of splashing creeks. We soon reached Patlanala and slowed down as we plodded into high, rough country along a steep, stony trail. My little skinny black mare was marvelously sure-footed, easy to manage, and eager to go. Dawn seeped over cactus and mesquite and barren crags. We took another level stretch at a gallop. But Eyler, some distance behind, called out in an anguished voice to stop while he fixed his stirrups, which were too short. After another stretch, he called out again and begged me to change horses with him. His sorrel was too difficult. So I won the toss, after all, but now was sorry to give up my own mount. Once more we readjusted the stirrups.

The sorrel was difficult. He had been a racer, and a racer's pace is disconcerting for steady travel. Given the slightest free rein, regardless of the terrain, he would dash ahead like the wind. To hold him in was to get a constant jolting. He was also a bad shyer, especially when racing; a piece of paper, a bush, a rock would cause him to leap to one side, and several times I almost went over his head. But he calmed down as the country got steeper and rougher. The trail was full of round loose stones, heartbreaking for any horse.

We plodded up a gypsum trail past Guastepec, set on a hill above a white church. Peasants trotted along, carrying big baskets of pitahaya cactus fruit on their heads. A bad rainstorm hit us, but the sun was out dazzlingly when we landed in hot San Francisco Paxtlahuaca among dense groves of twisted pitahaya trees that loomed up like giant candelabra.

The appointed mayor, an Indian with a sparse beard who barely spoke Spanish, was cordial. We chatted, squatting on the ground, in front of the town hall which was being re-decorated and was full of scaffolding. An elaborate fresco on the façade showed a train, a steamboat, and harbor, never seen by any resident of inland Paxtlahuaca, and was dedicated to a Napoleonic gentleman named Francisco Castillo who had inaugurated the building in 1929.

Everywhere throughout this semi-barren region folk invited us to eat the enormous scarlet pitahaya fruit, which tasted like a cross between raspberry and watermelon ice, plus a dash of some other flavor, and felt sandy on the tongue. The people all but live off their pitahaya forests, for water is scarce and their pitiful cornfields yield but little. Here, too, busy fingers shuttled constantly, weaving straw sombreros.

After a good bath in the river and a meal in the next village, where we ate in the town hall on a clothless table: eggs, chile, tortilla, coffee, and more pitahaya fruit, we pushed downstream to a little village which could be approached only by secret lanes through a cactus jungle in the fashion of a Minatoan maze. All through the revolution this place had escaped profanation, for only those knowing the secret paths ever stumbled upon it.

The country beyond was more open, fewer pitahaya groves, only a pincushion effect on the dusty plain and hills as far as the eye could reach. At San Agustín Atenango everybody was exceedingly cordial, particularly the lively schoolteacher, his pretty girl assistant, and the school-board president, a simple, kindly Indian. The portly pockmarked storekeeper set out free refreshments, a soft drink made from pitahaya and *nache*, a super-sweet cherrylike fruit. He was considered the educated man of the village and was regarded with awe because he subscribed not only to the

Excelsior in Mexico City but the magazine *Hacienda,* published in faroff New York City. He plied us with questions about that place.

The villagers complained bitterly of trouble with neighboring Coapala where the Indians were tough eggs. Not only did they constantly hack each other up in drunken machete fights, then cure the wounds by pouring on hot resin, but any outsider was lucky to get through the place unrobbed and alive. The Coapalans live on a straight milk-and-banana diet, refusing to eat meat, which would seem to refute the contention that all vegetarians are pacifists. Until a few years ago Mixtepec, another neighboring town, had been equally wicked, a den of bandits who boldly divided up their booty in the town hall. But a road had since been put through the town, and overnight it had become orderly and industrious.

Here we heard the legend of the founding of the original Mixtecan empire, and were shown pottery, grinding stones, and woodcarving with scenes from the epic story. A feathered Indian bearing a shield, bows and arrows, is shown planted arrogantly before the setting sun, the first Mixtec warrior to enter this upland plateau. He had been born of a majestic tree in Apoala canyon and was the progenitor of the whole Mixtecan race. Tired from the stiff ascent into the high country, his feet bruised by the sharp stones, his tormented imagination beheld the setting sun as the Lord of the region. "Not for a moment did the warrior's courage falter; protecting himself with his shield, he shot his arrows at the sun with all his strength. The horizon clouds turned red as blood, and the sun vanished into them, wounded unto death. The archer was victorious. The land was now his." The legend symbolizes the eternal struggle against the fierce heat and drouth of this barren homeland by a race long innured to hardship and poverty, a stern, determined people, never fully conquered by the Aztecs.

Hot, hot, hot was the road to Tonalá, a nondescript mestizo town, dismal, dilapidated, full of near-naked starving folk. We took a room in the dirty blue *mesón*, a miserable hole, though it had clean lace curtains. After a stroll down the garbage-littered main street we sat in the flyspecked parlor waiting for food. It took more than an hour just to get eggs. No meat was available. "It rots before it can be cooked," we were told.

At silver dawn we forded the river out of town. Birds were trilling and parrots shrilling in the high branches. In San Marcos, a prosperous little Indian town, we had a fine lunch of fried chicken. From here we took a short cut. Crossing a small stream, my horse floundered and sank. Soon the water was up to the pommel. Standing up on the saddle, I took a flying leap toward shore, praying I would get clear. Stones rolled under my feet, and I made shore. The horse, relieved of my weight, floundered a way downstream and managed to get free. Badly frightened, he tore off at a wild gallop, giving us a merry chase.

We descended into a broad valley through glistening fields and orchards and clean, prosperous settlements to Huajuapam de León, a town of 6,000 inhabitants. Mail was waiting for us at the post office. A card from Petra. All was well. They hoped I would be back soon. A letter from Magdalena. She had reached Tampico and was enjoying herself. There was another crazy, insulting card from Boak. Letters from the States. My agent. My publishers. Friends.

The place, though historic and picturesque, was a dilapidated dirty mess, but it has since been cleaned up considerably. The plaza was a tangle of weeds and refuse. The bandstand was tottering from dry rot; the school was utterly neglected; the city hall was cracking, the plaster falling off in chunks and the windows broken and filthy. For the only water supply for the entire city was the filthy plaza fountain. Fortunately our hotel brought in outside water on burros from the mountains, and the hotel was as clean and neat as any we had encountered in the back country.

The town, run down after so many decades of civil war, was now spending all its money on keeping up the church. At the moment the authorities were repairing and calcimining the half-moon-shaped wall around the yard, and the façade was painted a shrill blue. It was an extremely pious town, and the church bells, federal laws to the contrary, banged and bellowed from dawn until late at night. After five in the morning it was impossible to get any sleep.

The rainy season, earlier than usual, was now full upon us, quite in defiance of Eyler's long-forgotten schedule. Water came down in sluices, hour after hour, smashing loudly against walls and patio pavements, staining all the sky-blue calcimining a purple tinge, beating down the scarlet begonias and bougainvillaeas. We waited for a letup, but after a week decided we had to get out, rain or no rain. We were sick of the sight and smell of horses, and hoped we could hire a car.

Three roads led out of town, passable in the dry winter season, when regular passenger auto service is maintained north to the railway junction and east to a good highway connecting with Oaxaca City. These two routes were now definitely closed, no more service until late fall, but there was a chance we could still get through to Tehuacán, a winter resort on the railroad line. Though by far the worst road, it was high through sandy and rocky country. The car owner demanded sixty pesos for the trip, the customary rate for seven passengers, and was not at all eager to rent to us. But he guaranteed good tires, a good chauffeur, and gave us an iron-clad stipulation to get us to Tehuacán or not charge a penny. If all went smoothly, the trip would take fifteen hours. If we hit unusually heavy rains and had to wait for streams to subside, it might take two or three days.

We drummed up several stranded passengers to share costs and started out late the following morning in a day briefly free of rain. On the outskirts the chauffeur sneaked his girl into the car for companionship. She was having a free ride at our expense, but we thought it better to have his good will than object. Greater capacity for necking I have never yet beheld, and most of the way, though often the road went along dangerous cliffs, he paid little attention to his driving.

In places the road was little better than a goat track, and we had to knock down cactus and climb over incredible rocks. In lower, undrained valley stretches we floundered in mud. In one little valley we dug ourselves out of mud three times, and one slippery red-clay hill cost us hours of struggle and left us looking like circus clowns. In a low llano we struck mud bogs that finally turned into a lake for fifty yards. Our chauffeur explored possible ways to cut around through the fields, but vetoed the effort and said we had to drain the lake. For many hours we dug trenches and finally got the water running off. We carted in stones, gravel, and tree branches, and literally rebuilt the road.

On another occasion we had to detour through maguey fields for a quarter of a mile and found ourselves trapped beyond a deep gully. Our chauffeur drove inland over the hard sand soil, hoping to find a low place where he could cross. We finally had to cut a road down one bank and up another.

From here on we had a stretch of good going, although rain was now coming down in such torrents we could not see before our noses. We reached a large stream, still low but rising fast. We urged the chauffeur to try to get across without delay, but he shook his head mournfully and said we would wait till the rain let up. But it turned into a near cloudburst, and the car roof began to leak badly. Soon the river was much higher, but our driver then said rather than be stranded here, since there was a village not far distant on the other side where we could spend the night, he'd try to make it across. We were sure he had lost his chance to make it, and to lighten the car we all climbed out in the pelting rain. He backed up the road for a good stretch, then slammed into the water full speed and naturally stalled his engine—right in midstream.

We bellowed to some Indian shacks on the far bank, and for a few centavos the peasants carried us and our luggage across on their backs. After nearly an hour's walk through the slashing rain and wind we reached a forlorn little hill village. Not a light showed anywhere.

We forced our way into the schoolhouse, but the floor was a sea of mud, all the benches piled up in one corner. The town hall was locked and the doors too solid to be forced. No one was around, and the rain was coming down worse than ever. We finally stirred up a surly old peasant. He shrugged and said he had no idea where we could stay for the night.

"Where is the mayor?"

"He and most of the village are in the monte—out in the brush."

I gave the old codger half a peso and promised him another if he would bring the mayor in. He hobbled off muttering unpleasantly. We huddled around in the rain, but in about half an hour the mayor arrived, water streaming off his oilskin coat. He was in a nasty temper. A lean, sour-faced mestizo, he had precisely the racial mixture that seems to produce what is known as "a bad hombre." With ill grace he opened up the city hall, lit the carbide lamp, and read the letters we carried from the governors of Guerrero and Oaxaca and the minister of education.

He handed them back contemptuously. "This is neither Oxaca nor Guerrero. You are in the sovereign state of Puebla from the moment you crossed that river." Actually, we discovered that the rear bumper of the stalled car was in Oaxaca and the front in Puebla.

"That being the case," he snapped, "I don't have to do a blessed thing for any of you." He cursed the road, wished there wasn't any road. The village did not need or want outsiders coming through. People should have more sense than to travel this time of year, or any time. They shouldn't expect to bother the village and be helped out of difficulties. Automobiles were an abomination.

He finally consented ill-humoredly that we could sleep in the city hall if we would bar it well from the inside. He did not want anybody sneaking in and stealing things.

Our chauffeur asked for men to help get the car out. He feared it might be swept away by the rising waters.

"It's too dark now," snapped the mayor. "I won't risk anybody's life or comfort. Your car can sit there until tomorrow, and if it doesn't, it's not my worry, I can tell you."

"I'll hire some men myself."

"Tomorrow," roared the mayor. "No man moves a finger in this village without my consent."

"We'd like something to eat. We'll pay for it."

The mayor sent several idlers to inquire. A half-wit beggar was hanging to my coattails whining for pennies. His rags stank. It was worth something to get him away. I gave him twenty centavos to clear out and not bother us.

The mayor seized the half-wit by the scruff of the neck, twisted the money out of his hand, and stuck it in his own pocket. Soon the beggar was back, whining about his hard luck. A pretty community to have fallen into, run by a ruffian mayor who would steal twenty centavos off a beggar. But I decided it was best not to antagonize his ugly nibs.

In about half an hour we were called through the hammering rain to a store in a palm-thatched hut where we were given hot tortillas, chile, tough meat, and a brew that passed for coffee. The mayor accompanied us, and waited impatiently for us to finish. When we paid, he held out his hand and collected part of the money from the proprietor.

We undid our bags and unrolled our blankets. I announced I was going to get into dry things, but I had no privacy, even when I rubbed myself down with a towel. The chauffeur, his girl, the mayor, and a knot of curious bystanders watched the proceedings with interest. But mostly the mayor eyed our belongings greedily. If we weren't robbed and didn't have our throats cut this night we would be lucky.

I showed our idols from Silicayoapan to the town secretary. Everybody crowded around chattering excitedly in Mixtec. The secretary, holding the hermaphrodite idol in both hands, intoned singsong phrases and kissed it with slobbering lascivity. The idols seemed to make them more cordial. There was a note of suppressed excitement. Both the secretary and the mayor begged me to give them the idol. I made a vague half-promise, but had no intention of doing so.

We made a passable bed on the brick floor with grain sacks. We had to push everybody out bodily in order to get to sleep. Our sleep was not sound. The chauffeur and his girl were busy the whole night, and we gloomily predicted that on the morrow he would be so sleepy he would run us over a cliff.

We had hoped for an early start, for Tehuacán was still distant. The chauffeur came back from the river saying the river had gone down a few feet, the car was still there. But we still could get no help extracting it, and it was nine o'clock before we were able to get breakfast at the store. The townspeople who happened in were cordial and likable, erasing some of the evil impressions. But the mayor was still in a foul temper and made no move to help us and warned us not to try to hire anybody.

The sun wheeled high and hot. The mayor and his little gang sat sullenly apart in the plaza shade, obviously taking savage delight in making us wait and wanting the chauffeur to pay him a large sum. The villagers who helped us would not get a cent, the mayor would pocket it all.

About eleven the church bell rang, the signal to assemble the villagers. Our hopes rose, but it was merely to call them to work on the new curatage being built for the priest. This was obligatory communal labor.

Not till noon did the chauffeur and the mayor get around to haggling over price. About one o'clock a compromise was reached. Five pesos down and ten more when the car was fished out.

"It's a swindle," said the chauffeur. "Five pesos is even too much in a place like this."

But the mayor came to life with a bang and rushed villagers to the river. They carried the car ashore bodily. While this was going on I asked the mayor why they didn't fix up the school. Angrily he replied, "You can see everybody is busy on the curatage." He whetted a big knife in an ugly manner.

"But aren't your children just as important?"

He flew into a violent rage. "It's nobody's *chingado* business what we do around here!" There was an ugly echo from the Indians standing about.

Fortunately just then the car nosed into the plaza.

"Get your things aboard pronto," the chauffeur said in sotto voce. "We're moving out of this bandits' nest fast."

We piled in. "What's the idea?"

"That bandit mayor wants to clean us out. Those five pesos are all he's going to get."

The mayor jumped on the running board, demanding the ten pesos. The chauffeur argued that it was too much. He started the motor. "Want to put some water in the radiator," he said, "then I'll pay you."

We circled the cobblestone plaza ever more rapidly. The mayor was beginning to shout, "Don't think you'll get out of this town without paying."

As we neared the lane going east out of town, the chauffeur stepped on the gas, reached over, and slugged the mayor. With a terrific blast of his horn, he roared down the lane, hitting drains and gutters, sending chickens and pigs and children flying for safety. The mayor still hung on.

He yelled at us to stop, yelled at the chauffeur for bringing a whore into a decent town. The chauffeur called him a
cabrón and tried to slug him again. The mayor reached for
his throat, and the car swerved dangerously.

The girl dug her claws down the mayor's face. The
chauffeur pulled free and slugged the mayor on the nose.
We hit a deep ditch that threw us against the hood. The
mayor lost his grip and rolled head over heels into a bog
hole full of pigs. He struggled to his feet, his bleeding face
smeared, shook his fist, and shouted. But already, barely
missing a telegraph pole, we were well out of town.

A little farther on the chauffeur stopped to wipe the sweat
off his face. He looked around and grinned. "That's the first
time I ever rolled a mayor in the mud."

"Won't he make it hot for you when you return?"

"No, our line stands in with the commandants in Tehuacán and Huajuapan. I'll come back with a soldier. His nibs
won't dare touch me. Anyway, I won't come back till the
river is low, and I'll go through at sixty miles an hour with
my gun in hand."

"You're lucky he didn't stick his knife into you."

"The only way he'd stick a knife into you would be in
your back when you weren't looking. He won't last long.
The people in that village are going to pound his head in
with stones, wait and see."

The road steadily improved. It wound through picturesque, fertile country, with quaint towns and magnificent
churches set on the shoulders of hills. We reached the famous salt mines, and from here on we had a wide, well-
surfaced highway through high mountains, around hairpin
curves overlooking mighty abysses—but our chauffeur was
too busy kissing his girl to look where he was going.

At last we swung down to an enormous desolate plain on the far side of which rose the golden towers of Tehuacán. Late afternoon we drove up to an elegant hotel and strode, dirty and disheveled, through the tearoom to the lobby desk, just as the tropic rain flailed on the tinted glass skylight.

XIII

HOW TO FLIRT IN TEHUANTEPEC

IN rural Mexico, our ugly experience in the Puebla border town to the contrary, people are so hospitable it is hard to spend a cent, but in far southeast Tehuantepec, where the country pinches in to the narrow lowland isthmus, every man stuck out his palm insolently. "Give me a tostón [half a dollar]—Buy me a drink."

The mystery was soon cleared up. I looked like a candidate for Congress, who was blue-eyed and wore khaki and leggings as I did, and to the dark-skinned Tehuantepec folk, all Nordic types, like the Chinese to us, look alike. The candidate had appeared with bulging bags of silver tostones and had refused no man a drink. The blond candidate lost the election by only twenty-eight votes. I had churlishly refused about thirty people, so there is little doubt my untimely arrival blighted a promising political career. It was the nearest I have ever come to being an effective politician.

The rainy season had not hit Tehuantepec yet, but near there I ran into a bad locust plague, which always occurs on election year, thus revealing, even to the non-mystic soul, Nature's sublime coordination. The pests had stripped mountain and field utterly bare and flew by the train-car windows so thick we could not see out. Presently the train was stalled by the slippery rails. For some miles the train crew had to get out and throw sand on the track.

The pests and I—Eyler had returned to Mexico City—flocked into the sand-logged isthmus port of Salina Cruz. They covered every shrub inches deep and even converted palm fronds into dangling brown fibers. They devoured starched curtains and dresses, leaving some girls—the story was gleefully told—with only their metal stays before they could duck into their homes.

When I woke the next morning, though in spite of the intense heat I had left the window open only a crack, they were snuggled into bed with me, the tile floor was coated with them, the big brass spittoon looked like an animated Egyptian pyramid, and they were swimming in the water pitcher.

The military commandant rose to the occasion and fired off many salvos of artillery, a scientific experiment wholly successful; the pests, having eaten everything in sight, moved on to fertile Juchitán. The grateful Salina Cruz folk tendered the commandant a banquet and rang all the church bells. The angry Juchitecans sardonically sent a baked locust pie to him as their "respectful" contribution to the banquet.

Due to some recondite locust psychology, luxuriant Tehuantepec escaped the winged horde and was still an unmarred bower of tropical green and vivid flowers, where parrots chattered and redheaded zopilotes ruled over the public plaza. The vegetation was almost too lush—bananas, oranges, sour and sweet limes, grapefruit, melons, rubber trees, avocados, zapotes, breadfruit. There were scarlet acacias, oleanders, lilies of the valley, chrysanthemums, carnations, roses. The market cascaded with fruit and blossoms, golden mangoes, peaches, plums, chirimoyas, mameys, cherries.

The tall, handsome women of Tehuantepec, though barefoot, wear the showiest costumes in all Mexico. The lower half of their red or blue or yellow skirt is pleated lace, and when they carry jars or baskets on their heads, their long petticoats swing wide like bells over their shapely ankles. The flounces form and re-form in pleasing fluid designs, marking the line of the body, at other times mysteriously concealing it. Above their loose short-sleeved, low-cut blouses rises a convertible collar and bonnet of flexible pleats of stiffly starched lace. For everyday it lies low on exposed neck and shoulders; when the girls traipse into church, it is pulled into a pious white oval about round faces. On festive occasions it is lifted up behind like a spreading snow-white peacock's tail and quivers with every lovelorn sigh, every laugh, every stamp of anger. In the dances, those headdresses are like a shower of white petals drifting on a sea of music.

The short blouse is not fastened to the skirt so that whenever the arms are lifted, a strip of golden belly skin shows. When a Tehuana wishes to flirt, she artfully raises one shoulder, showing a patch of stomach, and some are really bold about it.

The women boss Tehuantepec with energy, vivacity, and passion. They do most of the work, all the buying and selling, hold the family purse-strings while pretending that their lazy hammock-lolling husbands are the masters. Daring, full of fire and fun, their tongues are spicy, and they have few inhibitions. Sexual relations, except for married women and the more respectable well-to-do Europeanized group about the plaza—the *gente de razón*—are free. Casual relations, called "marriages behind the door"—*ti'izi ga*—are not tabu nor does any stigma attach to children born of such contacts. In most of the barrios, or wards, as in some surrounding villages, a virgin is unmarriageable. A wife lacking prior experience is considered too much bother, and if she had already had a child or two, her chances of wedlock are improved, for then there is no question about her fertility, and fledglings, already on the way to becoming providers, are considered a dowry.

However, among the *gente de razón* and some Indians virginity is highly prized. The father drives off the suitor with hot words, even throws stones or brandishes a shotgun or machete. When hide-and-seek has gone far enough, the boy leaves a gift at the door: a chicken, calf, or goat, maybe a load of wood if he is poor. If the offering is taken inside, it is a sign parental wrath has subsided, and the boy's parents, grandparents, aunts, and uncles call en masse on the girl's relatives with professional *cago-olas* or "speech-makers" to haggle over terms. The girl's father aims to get as many worldly possessions from the boy's family as possible. The boy's relatives point out the girl's defects: knock knees, ugly eyes, stupidity, unreliability, bad cookery, and bad morals. The heated debate sometimes ends up in free-for-all fights, but if a successful agreement is reached, gifts and family visits are exchanged and a big engagement party is celebrated.

The wedding day is gay with "joy music" and fireworks, drinking, and dancing. The celebrants escort the pair to the bridal chamber and hang around, singing, making music, drinking, and shouting encouragement to the groom until the latter emerges to present his mother with a bloodstained handkerchief as proof of the bride's virginity. This is jealously guarded in a carved gourd along with red hibiscus flowers to disprove any future slander. If the handkerchief cannot be produced, the girl is sent back to her parents then and there in disgrace. Some have been known to commit suicide.

In the morning the groom's family sends around girls with trays of hibiscus flowers which are given to neighbors in church and market as a formal announcement that the bride was "pure."

In some wards and villages trial marriages for six months or a year are celebrated. The girl lives with the boy's family. If she never talks back to her future mother-in-law, and proves to be a good washer, mender, weaver, and cook as well as agreeable bed companion, she is considered fit for the trials of matrimony, and marriage is solemnly celebrated with elaborate fiestas.

In one village, when a girl comes from the river with a water jar on her head, the suitor jumps out of the thicket and smashes it with a stick, drenching her, then tries to tear off her garments. Her girl friends rush to protect her, fighting him off with stones, sticks, and fingernails. If he is routed, he is considered a no-account and the courtship wanes. If he succeeds in stealing all her clothes, the father is required to grow angry over the disgrace and demands the return of her apparel. He goes around with a gun or knife telling the world he intends to kill the insolent scamp, but presently banns are posted and marriage wipes out the "insult" of pretended rape.

In another remote town farther up the coast I went to a marriage supper in which a turkey was let loose with cigarettes tied to its feathers. There was a grand hilarious melee as the guests tried to yank them loose. Little plumage was left on the poor screaming bird. The bride next came in with cigarettes sewed on her blouse and skirt and after another hilarious scramble, she too, was left with little plumage, only a few tatters. She and the groom were then rushed to the bridal chamber, and the guests serenaded their love-making all night with instruments and bawdy songs.

In Tehuantepec customs vary from barrio to barrio. Each ward has its own patron saint and elders. Social life consists in inviting friendly wards to big fiestas and dances or to saints' days. Each guest first greets the elders, who always preside seated Turk fashion on a long mat. Prolonged formalized courtesies about the weather, health, crops, animals, and new babies are exchanged. The guests express great admiration for the paper-flower decorations and the great honor of being invited. They make a small monetary donation to help cover the cost of refreshments and music, and each guest is then given a special drink of fiery mescal, several cigarettes, and a tissue-paper flag for his hat to show that he has paid. Women pay a smaller amount, and are given aromatic leaves and flowers to put in their hair.

Such fiestas start with daybreak songs under the windows, either the Zapotec "dawn song" or Spanish "mañani-

tas," to wake people sweetly. According to the nature of the
fiesta, special music is played, "The Sweet Sugar Cane"
song, "The Fruit-Throwing" song, the "Hummingbird" or
"Jaguar" or "Lizard" song. The fishermen's barrio has its
own special music, "The Sword Fish" song, "The Crocodile"
tune. Morning hours are given over to old-fashioned folk
dances in which even grandmothers take part, usually the
son, a modified waltz in which partners do not touch bodies
and whirl wide. The favorite *son* is the Zandunga "Beautiful Girl." The chanted verses go back for centuries.

> Curly-headed girl with the black eyes! My, oh, my!
> Lips of parted coral, heaven of my heart,
> Take me into your loving arms. My, oh, my!
> Let me sleep there, heaven of my heart!

> *Chorus:*
> Ay Zandunga! What a gold Zandunga!
>   My, oh, my!
> Zandunga for whom I weep,
>   Jewel of my Heart.

This swirling dance shows off the fine silks and velvets,
the vivid embroidery, and the shimmering lace of the costumes, the quivering headdresses. Nothing is more stunning
than the mellowed flame of tropic light falling through the
wattled walls on glowing colors.

In the afternoon the younger folk snuggle close to dance
modern jazz, blues, rumbas, and the precise passionate
danzón. Mostly, however, the step is a jerky waltzlike movement of bare feet on hard-packed dirt floor, skirts flying out
in wide arcs, a flaming whirl till the head grows woozy.

Amorous fingers creep in between skirt and blouse to the smooth, soft skin; whispered love brings flushed cheeks and sparkling eyes.

Each barrio has its own handicraft specialty or occupation, though all grow corn, beans, and other crops. Some paint gourds with rich floral and animal designs. Others weave, embroider, sell fish, make jewelry or pottery. "The thieves' barrio" is a tough quarter. Among its murky cactus lanes anybody is apt to be held up or get a knife in his ribs. The police rarely interfere with the customs of the various barrios, and merely shrug, for no outsider with the least sense would venture into the thieves' barrio after dark, but let the thugs ply their trade one foot out of this restricted area, and they are likely to end up before a firing squad in short order.

The hotel was presided over by an enormous Spanish lady in an elegant red-brown velvet costume. She was always coy with her patch of stomach skin. In the dining-room terrace, shaded by fine trees, one of the guests was one of the most beautiful Tehuanas I had yet seen. She was with a Mexican, obviously from the capital, and I wondered how this outsider had so quickly netted such a choice native girl. After lunch, he got out a drawing board and began making a sketch of Coney Island, an Italian with a great swarm of offspring overflowing a roller coaster high in the air.

At once I knew this must be Miguel Covarrubias, at that time doing illustrations for *Vanity Fair*. "*Buenos días*, Don Miguel," I ventured.

He was surprised but cordial. The beautiful Tehuana was his wife Rosa, a dancer, wearing the local costume and tanned by the sun.

I moved from the hotel to a roomy thatched home under false peppers high on the river bluff, a family of three sisters who wove cloth and made costumes. Every afternoon, about our teatime, they stopped their work, friends dropped in to chat, and hot chocolate was served. The thatched terrace gave a fine vista of the winding river, distant cornfields, and jungle. The river was always busy with animals coming to drink, fishermen in loincloths, oxcarts crossing, boatmen leisurely poling upstream, and, at all hours except during hot siesta time, nude bathers of both sexes, each in a designated locale.

Getting a bath in Tehuantepec is not easy. The hotel had showers. The only public facilities were the river and the baños dobles or double-baths. At the double-baths they ask you if you have a female companion or wish one provided. The person who bathes alone is considered "queer." Hot water is poured over red-hot stones providing dense gagging steam. An old Indian woman throws bucket after bucket of icy water over you; she, or your *compañera*, if you prefer, rubs you down and thumps you.

Often I bathed in the river, feeling overnaked because of my white skin, which excited comment until I tanned up. One afternoon a portly American woman with tallow freckled arms came down in a gold-colored bathing suit. The men rolled with laughter, but the naked local girls showed great indignation. "*Gringa indecente*," they shrilled. "Look at the lewd American woman making a dirty show of herself in a swim suit."

One day, sitting on the bank watching the girls bathe, which is considered quite proper, I focused my kodak on them. Angry shouts arose. A stone whizzed past my ear. The girls swarmed up the riverbank pelting me with stones, and I had to take to my heels, that whole crew of nude women in full bay behind me. Though I am aware of the fate of Lot's wife, I have always regretted I was in too much of a hurry to look back.

Tehuantepec has a movie, ice plant, electric lights, telephone, and telegraph, and a railway station several miles out, also an air strip, but otherwise is unmechanized save for a machine in the market where women get their lye-soaked corn ground into masa for tortillas, which saves endless hours of work at a grinding stone and has the advantage of having no human sweat mixed in. One modern gadget, besides revolvers, that is most prized is a sewing machine with pleater attachment because of the innumerable pleats that go into each lace costume. Every Tehuana schemes to get money to make her first payment on a machine.

A local lovelace discovered that the easiest way to any woman's heart was to own a sewing machine. By such bait he enticed many a fair one to his house, even uncorrupted respectable matrons. The Casanova had to be curbed. As Tehuantepec is somewhat civilized, he was not tarred or feathered or gelded. One dark night Vigilantes threw his sewing machine into the river.

In the market I often sipped a tamarind refresco at the stall of Matilda, a handsome young widow. An old crone was seated on the curb crocheting. She chuckled and said slyly from her toothless mouth, "Young foreigner, you have been in Tehuantepec more than a week now, why haven't you gotten yourself a steady girl? There are so many beautiful ones, you need not look far."

"It would be too bad to make a mistake."

The old crone's lace headdress quivered mirthfully. "If you got a giddy, inexperienced girl there might be risk if it

were for more than a night's pleasure, but Matilda here"
—she waved her gnarled fingers to the widow—"is ripe and
sweet and knows everything necessary to make a bed a
happy place." The old crone cackled. "She's a good worker
so you would have no worry except keeping your hammock
comfortable, nor would you have to keep an eye on her
every moment like most. She's intelligent and chock full of
fun and would give you more juice and joy than some un-
tried one. Could you ask for more?"

Matilda busied herself in the stall, paying no heed to such
nonsense.

"Matilda," I answered gallantly, "would be a prize for
any man."

"And you, Matilda?" persisted the crone, "don't fiddle
and flounce as though you hadn't heard me. Would you take
the *guero*, the blond one?"

Matilda's pretty black eyes looked me over insolently,
and she flipped her blouse, showing her golden belly, an
honor, for she rarely bothered to flirt, though many buzzed
hopefully around her counter. "Why not, pray tell?" she replied, with a cheerful nod.

"There you have it," chortled the crone. "It's all arranged."

Matilda lifted her shoulder to give me another generous
skin peep. "The Señor is worth marrying, but he's an outsider and sooner or later will leave Tehuantepec and I
would have to go with him. But not even for him, no not
even for a bullfighter, will I ever leave Tehuantepec. Why
should anyone ever leave Tehuantepec?"

I have yet to find a suitable answer to that question.

XIV

SAY IT WITH CALLA LILIES

"You are back! God be praised!" cried Petra.

I gave them all an abrazo and told them how much I had missed them.

"The Señor was very good to write to us, but even without that you would have found the house scrubbed and clean."

When I hugged Lupe, I asked how transportation was these days, and her black eyes flashed.

"She's getting more sense," said Petra. "But María . . ."

María swung on one heel and twisted at her dress. "She and Gabriel are very much in love."

"His intentions are honorable, I suppose."

"Love is always honorable."

Mario, I think, was the happiest of all to have me back. "Any *special* thing you want done?" he said with a grin, and I gave him an affectionate cuff.

I rushed around town, sniffing at every corner. Rosalinda was taking the sun in front of El Morenito. "Did you find many *simpaticas* on your trip?" she teased.

"None to equal Rosalinda."

"Go on with you. I know all about those shameless pretty Tehuanas."

Carmen at her orange stand beamed. "You will want your two oranges as usual?"

"Of course."

"You are very tanned, señor. You're almost a *prieto*—a dark one—like the rest of us."

Don Nacho's long legs were stretched across the sidewalk as though he had not moved an inch since I had last seen him. I tossed the usual coin into his sombrero.

He held it toward me with an aggrieved look. "I'm sorry, señor, but you owe me two pesos and twenty-five centavos."

"I *owe* you?"

"*Pues sí, señor.* You were gone forty-five days and not one of those days did you give me the five centavos upon which I depend greatly."

"But if I had never come back?"

"It is well known in Coyoacán that you would."

For a place without a newspaper Coyoacán does pretty well. I shelled out.

This was Thursday, so I went to Don Pepe's for lunch. Everybody thumped my shoulders and asked about my trip. I had hit a dramatic day. During my absence, Don

Miguel had up and married his mistress, the cantina girl, and she would be here for lunch.

Pepe had been worried that this might happen. "We all have our little love nest, young or old, but there's no reason for him to marry that little rag. His sweet cousin, Refugio, is a beautiful girl with a big dowry. She loves the dumpy frog, and he could have her by snapping his fingers. But no, he has to pick up with a cheap tramp."

Now it had happened without warning. A prolonged family council had been held, and after all the pros and cons were in, Grandmother Leonor, as head of the household, made the decision from which there was no appeal. "We shall regret it always if we are not nice to her. We would lose Miguel, and everybody would be unhappy. She must be treated as one of the family, the newest, most honored member of the family. What she did before is nobody's difference, and those of our friends who can't accept her can stay away. I shall not tolerate the slightest affront to her from anybody in our family or out of it."

Isabel did not give in without a bit more argument. Leonor told her sharply that among upper-class Mexicans a divorcée, as Isabel had been, and an opera singer, were not accepted. "I was the one who decided you should be taken in as a social equal."

Isabel said no more and promptly called on Catalina with an expensive present and invited her to this lunch to which all close friends of the family were asked to come. Pepe gave her a costly diamond clip and bought new furnishings for their home. He opened his arms, his heart, and his purse.

She came in with Miguel, scared stiff, rather pathetic with faded blond hair, a flabby handshake, and a beaten-up look. It was hard to imagine she had ever had the flair to be a cabaret girl, though she had a smooth golden skin and was nicely shaped. She was installed on Pepe's right and everybody was attentive until they realized it embarrassed her. Under the cloak of the noisy conversation, Pepe thawed her out, their heads were soon close together in laughter. Tubby, froglike Pepe always had a way with the ladies.

The guest of honor, other than Catalina, was Federico Gamboa, a dignified old-school gentleman, a brilliant professor, playwright, and the author of *Santa*, a best-selling novel about a prostitute. Another playwright present was my friend Raul Granados, a diplomat temporarily in disfavor. Much of the table talk centered on personalities in the theater: Lupe Vélez, whose navel jelly dances in three roses and a smile were the talk of the town. María Conesa, "The Little Gold Cat," the clever Spanish singer and dancer, on whom the minister of agriculture had been lavishing gifts. Repeatedly she had shaken the capital with scandal; once had been involved as the recipient of a stolen pearl necklace given to her by a general who manipulated the "Gray Automobile Gang," robbing wealthy residences. The government had hastily shipped him off on a European commission, and the members of the gang were then liquidated by "suicides" and "mortal fights" in prison before the case ever came to trial. Though now about fifty, she was as popular as ever on the stage and had gotten her golden claws into the president's private secretary. In order to get money for her palatial residence, jewels, and milk baths, he had promoted a private smuggling ring and had forged the president's signature permitting goods to enter duty free. He was pulled down in disgrace and María Conesa presently was exiled from Mexico forever.

There was Delia Magaña, lively hoyden comedian, at the

moment in the throes of a passionate love interest in a prominent Hollywood actor, who had invited her north to Hollywood. When he left the city, Delia had been unable to get off from her act at the Lírico Theater, but right after the show she had secured a siren police car and a motorcycle escort and blazed through the city a sixty plus to catch up with the train at the Tacubaya suburb, just in time to jump aboard and kiss him good-by.

At a Sunday dinner where I was present with her, she said—she knew only a few words of English—"I luff many men, but *many* men. Then Griffith, he come. ZOOM!" she jabbed her forefinger into her heart.

Another time I came upon Delia under less pleasant circumstances. I was walking along Avenida Juárez, with Noriega Hope, a journalist on *El Universal*, also a playwright, when Larry Crawford (let us call him that), an American correspondent, grabbed my arm and insisted I have a drink with him. He was already half-seas over. He was always impossible when he was drunk, either effusively affectionate or bellicose. It was impossible to refuse him; the only way was to accept his drink, then duck out at the first chance. This time he dragged me around the corner to the blue-tiled Regis bar.

There in a booth in a hilarious party were Delia and several other Lírico strip teasers with a general and his cronies, and the general was none other than "the killer" who disposed of enemies of the regime by assassinations and *ley de fuga*. Soon Larry insisted on intruding into their party in spite of my efforts to pull him away. Delia finally burst out, "Go way, dirty American pig!" Larry's reply caused the general's hand to move toward his gun. I dragged Larry off by force and got him into another booth. His one obsession now was to go back and clean up the whole party. There was every chance he would get killed.

I bribed the worried waiter to keep him in the booth by force if necessary and rushed out. Fortunately I found a policeman across the street. I slipped him a couple of pesos to go in and arrest Larry. He was then to walk him past the Alameda to Tío Pépé's bar, a place Larry liked where he always found boon drinking companions. I watched from under the park trees.

Presently the policeman came out hauling Larry roughly, for he was protesting and fighting, shouting that no Mexican policeman could arrest an American. The policeman followed my instructions, and pretty soon Larry was walking along with his arm about the policeman's shoulder in the most friendly style. Thinking all was well, I went on home to bed.

But about dawn I got a call from Larry's wife. Larry was in jail, could I help get him out? She had already called the American Embassy and the consulate.

I dressed hurriedly. Apparently Larry had grown ugly toward the policeman again, and in exasperation the latter had hauled him off to jail, where Larry had sat all night trying to read Wood's *Heavenly Discourse*, which he happened to have in his pocket. When I got to the jail, he was already out. His wife had paid over a hundred pesos, the fine which would be assessed for disorderly conduct, and they had let him off. I never did confess my responsibility in the matter because I may well have saved his life.

Now at the Calderón table, everybody agreed that the greatest Mexican comedian was Roberto Soto, another Lírico actor, built like Falstaff, who wrote his own skits in racy vernacular. His political satires infuriated whatever government was in power, but he was so popular that he was never bothered, and only once in his long career was one of his productions suppressed, and that caused such a furor that the government hastily backed water.

One night late I was chatting with a friend in the Alameda behind the big marble semicircular monument to Benito Juárez, Mexico's Lincoln, the hero of the mid-century reform movement. Don Roberto Soto lumbered along the sidewalk in front, on his way home after his show. In a deep, sepulchral voice I called out, "*Buenos noches,* Don Roberto."

The actor looked around but saw no one. Gravely, with exaggerated deference, he lifted his big Texas hat to the marble bust of the dead president. "*Buenos noches,* Don Benito." I later heard that he believed that the hero had actually spoken to him from the tomb.

After the customary post-meal entertainment in the sala I danced with Leonor, Isabel, then several times with Catalina. It was easy to tell she loved dancing better than anything else. Just before the guests left, Isabel put her arm around her and led her over to the piano to sing. And so pretty, pathetic little Catalina was duly installed with all honor in the great Calderón clan.

Quite some time before this I had met D. H. Lawrence and his wife Frieda numbers of times at the Monte Carlo Hotel, a shabby little hostelry near the National Library, where I often went to see Don Aurelio. Frieda was a buxom, Teutonic type, healthy, earthy, like home-baked bread, and Lawrence, who was sick and irritable, apparently frustrated by her health and calm, used to rail at her in language no man would use even to a harlot. But his irritation, always so palpable in his writings, apparently provided a certain anguished vision and mystical fear that always imparted to them a degree of originality and insight, however badly written.

Once he remarked, "The only place my books sell is in the United States, but that's because I'm a fad with an arty circle. At least the Englishmen who do read me understand what I'm trying to say."

He found it difficult to get along with anybody, though for some reason he was always friendly and considerate with me. Once he flew into a rage because a cabinet minister had asked me to postpone a dinner in his honor. Lawrence shouted angrily he wasn't going to stand on his head for any little Mexican cabinet minister and never did go to the dinner or send excuses. One day he grossly insulted a young American journalist I had brought to see him because the lad worshiped his writing. It was so uncalled for that I never went back to see him.

It was about this time, if I recall correctly, that I also met Somerset Maugham at the Hotel Regis, in a dinner party at the bar. Maugham was curious about the waiter, who had a dreadful scar down his face, and presently he was inventing a story to account for the injury and he got us all started on inventing similar yarns. Some were quite dramatic and original. After that Maugham could not rest until he found out how the injury had actually happened. As tactfully as I could, I asked the waiter. It was quite simple. A case of fizz water had blown up in his face. Maugham, I believe, later wrote this story much as it occurred, giving the various yarns, and making the whiplash the simple anticlimax of the truth.

During the evening I happened to ask if he would see D. H. Lawrence while he was in Mexico. He began to stutter worse than usual. "Is he in Mexico? He's one man

I never want to see again. I shall leave Mexico at once."

But Mexico is a big country, I said, and he replied, "No country is big enough to hold that creature and me."

He left very shortly, though he had planned a long stay.

Just before dinner, after my visit to the Calderóns, I stood looking at my garden. It was in bad shape. The beets had turned into pumpkins, the cabbages had gone to seed, the corn had become the forest primeval. The flower garden was certainly ragged. José was still numbered among the missing, but I had learned that it was tactful never to make any inquiries of Petra. I suspected we would never see him again.

At the meal I poked at the side dish. "What on earth is this?"

She laughed. "Your chayotes, señor."

"You mean . . ."

"I told you they kept indefinitely if put on the roof, and then they are much better."

"You can take it away."

Mario appeared lugging a large one and asked me to make him another jack-o'-lantern. I told him to do it himself, the way he would like it to look. He gave it a much more ferocious aspect than I had.

"Petra, do you remember David, the jewel merchant, and his plump sweetheart, Mary? They are getting married tomorrow."

This was one reason I had hastened back from my trip. When I reached the church on San Juan Letrán Street, Mary was already there, looking like a sweet, rosy, oversized cherub. Kate, who was to be bridesmaid, showed up in a lavender dress. The church was massed with flowers.

But David failed to appear. Half an hour passed; every-

body grew restless; but Mary smiled sweetly and confi-
dently. "It's just like David."

But when another quarter hour slipped by even Mary
became worried lest something had happened to him. The
minutes ticked on to a full hour, and presently it looked as
if he had left her high and dry. At the very end, after hand-
ing over her savings to him, she had been jilted. But she did
not give up faith. "If David is all right, he will get here,"
she repeated with apparent confidence.

The priest finally told her he had to leave because of
other pressing duties. Mary then broke down and sobbed in
Kate's arms. Kate wanted to take her home. "Not yet. Not
yet," Mary sobbed.

Just as Kate was leading her out, an enormous bunch of
calla lilies appeared at the church door. The lilies moved
forward as if propelled by themselves, then a pair of short,
plump legs in pin stripes showed beneath them. Down the
aisle came the lilies and the legs. Near the altar David's
round face emerged from the lilies. Mary almost fainted
with relief and joy.

He thrust the lilies into her arms and fell on his knees,
kissing the hem of her bridal gown. "Mary darling, forgive
me. I love you." His anguish was terrible and almost funny.

Mary held him in her arms and laughed and sobbed.
Everybody's eyes were wet.

What had actually happened was, that David's frock suit
had not come back from the tailors. He could not bear the
thought of getting married in an ordinary suit, and had
rushed all over town trying to locate the tailor who had
closed up shop for some family reason. Finally he borrowed
a suit from a friend. It didn't quite fit him. But we learned
none of this until long afterward. He claimed he had been

delayed because he felt he could not come to church without bringing Mary more flowers. Was it his belief, as usual, that poetry was more truthful than humdrum truth? Or a false sense of dignity?

We caught the priest, and the ceremony was duly performed. Both Kate and I still had lingering doubts whether such an odd alliance would be successful. It was all rather ludicrous but somehow touching and beautiful.

Several weeks later I was awakened by a commotion in the patio, just as my neighbor's "Anchors Aweigh" began playing. Gabriel's praying burro was peering through the laced brick parapet, his ears laid back. Astride him was perched María in her Sunday best, a red ribbon in her hair. Her dress, high on her knees, showed her twisted thin legs encased in silk stockings. She was surrounded by bags and bundles, and Petra rushed to her with a package of tortillas.

"A trip, María?" I asked.

She turned red. "Sí, señor."

"Without telling me good-by?"

"*Pues*, señor," she stammered. "I did not want to wake you up."

"What an idea!"

"We didn't know how you would take it. I go to live at Gabriel's house beyond the Pedregal."

"Then I shall kiss the bride."

"There has been no wedding, señor. We cannot do things as you would, for to get a priest and buy all the clothes and food and drinks for a wedding would cost more than we have."

Gabriel came over from where his burros were chewing my latest chayote vine.

"You've gotten a fine rascal, María. And you, Gabriel, are

getting a fine wife. She has been so good and loyal and has worked so faithfully, I was thinking of marrying her myself."

She giggled. "Me, señor! The Señor always likes his little joke."

"We love you and shall miss you, María. And you, Gabriel, are a sly wretch for stealing her this way."

He took off his sombrero and scratched his head. He patted the burro affectionately, this ferocious-looking pirate, and said gently, "I have given her little Diego for her very own. He's the dearest thing I own, but he's all hers now."

"I haven't had a chance to buy you two a present." I gave them ten pesos. Both remonstrated, and I added sternly, "Gabriel, I shall expect you to bring her along when you deliver our charcoal."

His black eyes in his sooted face turned into two lit candles. "If she wishes, señor. Only we would not want to bother you."

"I'm leaving on another horseback trip soon, but when I get back we shall have a big party for you both." I hesitated, not knowing if I was treading safe ground. "Would you like me to have the priest in?"

He scratched his head, frowning. "Nothing better would we like, but it costs too much for now. . . . The clothes and all."

"Wear the clothes you have on now. As for the priest, it will cost you nothing. That will be my real wedding present, if you would like it that way."

"That I would like better than anything, señor. Is it not the truth, María?"

He rounded up his burros, tugged villainously at his red sash, and they clattered off along the cobbles of Ave María, past El Morenito, and vanished into the gray, topsy-turvy

Pedregal. He made an extra show of guiding and shouting at his burros.

I stared at my new chayote vine. "Gabriel's burros always play havoc with it, don't they?" I said to Petra.

Her eyes filled, she flounced her skirts, and scolded Mario. Then she drew her *rebozo* over her head and fled sobbing to the kitchen.

XV

ADIÓS

OUR train wound up the narrow Cañada from Oaxaca toward Puebla, the city of blue tiles. On this trip I had ridden into the Mazateca regions of western Oaxaca into lofty villages where in several instances no living inhabitant had ever seen a white man before.

In Coyoacán Petra gave a glad call. "Mario! . . . Mario!"

She gave me news that María was happy. Lupe was away again, once more working at the Mexico City arms factory. There were other changes. The blond artist and her girl friends next door had departed. Walter Bailey and his wife

202

and sister were also gone. But Rosalinda was in the sun before her shop. Nacho's long legs stretched across the sidewalk. My bill was bigger than ever. Carmen, my orange
lady, was gone, having bought a stall in the Mercedes market in the city. But Niña, my flower lady, pressed a bunch of
gladiolas into my arms, to celebrate my return.

The next morning, when I heard "Anchors Aweigh," it almost seemed as if I had not been gone at all—a queer col-
lapsing of time and experience as though neither really ex-
isted. I was at my typewriter, racing to catch up with things,
when Mario ran to open the front door. Antonio and Marta
came in. She was carrying a bundle in a sky-blue blanket. A
chubby old man's face peered up at me with crinkled brown
eyes.

"It can't be possible." I counted on my fingers.

"You'll get no scandal out of your finger counting," Marta
said.

I looked at my second rampant chayote vine. "It seems
impossible, but time, I'm more convinced than ever, is purely
a psychological illusion. Why haven't I heard from you?"

"We've been happy and busy with the store, and now, the
baby. Yes, time depends on what you feel and what you are
doing. I can recall the mornings and afternoons when I used
to sit in the balcony on the avenue when we used to speak
to each other sometimes. I had only dreams and hopes those
days, often the hours went by very slowly. Now, I scarcely
have time to wash my face, but it is better this way."

Antonio broke in. "We want to know if you will be god-
father for"—he paused—"little Carletón Suárez."

"What! Poor tike! With that name he won't know which
handle to grab for."

"It's a fine name," said Marta.

"What on earth will the little fellow do in this country without a saint's name? He won't have even a saint's day."

"We'd like to have him baptized here in Coyoacán."

"I'll be fattening up the turkey."

Thursday noon I went to Pepe Calderón's. Catalina had lost her timid, beaten-about look and was quite a society matron now. I went on into the city with Raul Granados. He gave me tickets for his new play, *The Golden Pheasant,* opening at the María Consea Theatre.

Near the Zócalo I ran into Kate and asked her about David and Mary. "It's the strangest thing. Since their Vera Cruz honeymoon, no one has caught a glimpse of them."

"Latins like to keep their women locked up. No news is good news, I presume."

I dragged Don Aurelio out of the National Library for a game of chess.

Gradually I caught up with things, lunched with Edda, who had come back from the States, and invited her to the baptism. I looked up Howard Phillips, editor of *Mexican Life,* saw the Nutters, went to a party at the apartment of Frances Toor, editor of *Mexican Folkways.*

One fine morning I decided to hike across the Pedregal to see how María and Gabriel were getting along. It was not easy going over trails scarcely legible in the topsy-turvy lava, through fantastic formations, and down into little hollows. In spots where a few feet of soil had accumulated I stumbled upon little thatched huts, with a few corn stalks, goats, and pigs. Now and then a scrubby false pepper was able to take root in some crevice. Cactus flourished everywhere.

Gabriel's adobe house was located on a few acres of good land almost surrounded by lava flow. I would have known it, even if it had not been described to me, by little praying Diego, who was decked out with ribbons on his ears. The house was inside a tight organ cactus fence, and two eucalyptus trees towered high above it.

"The tax collector is here," I called through the cactus.

Tall Gabriel burst out, and we exchanged an *abrazo*. María came running. They introduced me to Gabriel's mother, a pleasant portly soul.

They wanted to kill the fatted calf for me, but I said I had no time, only for the tequilita Gabriel served me from a well-hoarded bottle. He told me about his life, not an easy one, for he had to go high up on the flanks of Ajusco to prepare his charcoal, bring it down, then peddle it across the Pedregal. But they were happy. María had put on a little weight, which became her.

I told them I had come about the fiesta, which would have to be fairly soon for I was going back to the United States. "I've already talked with Father Xavier. And you will come, too, Mamcita," I told Gabriel's mother.

"Ay, my bones are no good for such a trip."

"Nonsense. It's not so far to the lane, and a car can get through."

I headed back, for that evening Marta's and Antonio's baby was to be baptized. Plans had been changed. The ceremony would occur near their place in Colonia del Valle.

Their small modern apartment was packed with relatives, all sitting around solemnly, as usual the families of either side eying each other with a hint of hostility, but politer than usual. Drinks were served—such things cost a pretty penny.

Few would see the actual ceremony in the church, not even Marta, who was supposed to stay home to look after the guests. I protested that this was a barbarous idea, but they laughed at me and said, "It is the custom."

Antonio, his sister to hold the baby, a brother, and a superior at the railroad where he worked, plus the *padrinos,* or godfathers, Edda and myself, went to the parish house.

A pleasant young priest officiated. He wrote down the customary data in the church ledger. At the name "Carleton" he paused. "Very odd. I've heard of Charles and Carl in English, but never 'Big Carl.'"

The prefix "ton" in Spanish increases the size of the object. Thus *"cachete"* is cheek, and *"cachetón"* is a big, hanging jowl. I explained to the priest that it was really a surname. I had been named after a poet very popular when I was born, one "Will Carleton." "But I must warn you and the parents before they insist on the name that he was a very bad poet."

For a moment the priest was taken aback, then he smiled. "But perhaps he was a good man if his poetry was popular, and who knows maybe having such a name will inspire this child not only to grow into a good man but a really good poet."

The infant did not scream when the cold water was poured on the back of his head but gurgled with glee and tried to catch the silver stream in his hands. His amazing *sang-froid* was the chief topic of conversation over the tamales and atole that were served after we got back to the apartment.

"Where are the waffles?" I asked Marta.

"You're a good Mexican now."

"I suppose by the time I have another chayote vine there will be another little one."

"Not so fast. We aren't that old-fashioned any more."

The relatives, especially Antonio's, acted very shocked.

Since I would soon be leaving, I went into the city the next day and called on various friends. On Isabel la Católica Street I stopped dead in my tracks. There, in the block given over to antique shops, jewelers, and money-changers sat Mary Grant behind a brass cage in a breezeway. She was busily changing pesos into dollars and pounds.

"Mary! You have deserted all your friends. But married life seems to agree with you." She was blooming with health and good cheer. "Or is it having your fingers on so much coin of the realm?" What a change, I was thinking, for a one-time missionary.

"We've thought about you often, but I live in such a different world now that few of my American friends would understand, and every minute has been full—and deliriously happy."

She told me how they had set up housekeeping and had been kept busy entertaining David's numerous friends. "Several times he was so rushed, I came here to help out and discovered I have a knack for this. At first the idea of my working upset him dreadfully, but he has saved face by saying that since I am an American girl, it's all right, and now he's proud of the arrangement. It gives him time to carry on more jewelry business, so we are prospering."

"It's quite a change for you."

"This is better. I don't have to hide my real feelings and be nice to people just because they donated money. And David, believe it or not, he's a model husband. I never knew what it was to live until now."

And so all the Cassandras had been confounded. All the cards had seemed stacked against Mary, but she had held a royal flush and none of us knew it. She promised to try to get

David if he weren't away to come to my farewell party.
The Mendizábals gave me quite a send-off. A banquet was
to be served at midnight, but a few minutes before one of
the servants running in and out with dishes suddenly decided to have her baby. It arrived promptly less than half
an hour later, right on top of my hat on the bed. The house
was temporarily in confusion, and we did not sit down to eat
until two in the morning. As for the girl, when I went back
two days later to get my hat, she was up and around and
working, her baby in her arms.

The marriage fiesta demanded great preparations. Lupe
took a week off from the munitions plant to help, and she
and Petra and Mario scarcely had hands or feet enough to
tend to everything.

I bought the flowers. *"Buenos días,* Niñita," I said to my
buxom flower "baby" in the market. Her name I knew by
now was Doña Paz. "You have a fine name, 'Peace.' That is
what the world never values too much until it is lost. How is
it you don't have a saint's name?"

"My parents used to fight terribly, and they hoped my
coming would bring them peace."

"Did it work that way?"

"No, they fought worse than ever."

"But you are so peaceful and kind."

"Si, señor. My husband, Abraham, and I never quarrel."

"Don't you get bored?"

"Never, señor. We have too much fun with flowers, he
raising them and gathering them on the milpa and I selling
them. How can one get angry when one works with flowers?
And our five children are just like flowers to us."

Just then Abraham and a small boy trotted in with baskets
of calla lilies on their backs, held with straps across their

foreheads. Their brown faces shone in great white halos. Everything was ready, the house decorated, the big brown bowls in the kitchen simmering with food, the punch was made, and a mariachi orchestra was already tuning up in a corner of the patio. Guty Cárdenas had come to play his guitar. Petra had on a new dress and her rooster brooch. Mario's communion suit was spotless. Lupe wore red rayon like a dancing flame.

An auto sounded its horn. Gabriel came in resplendent in tight striped ranchero trousers that buckled under his new shoes. He grimaced slightly when he walked because never in his life had he worn anything but sandals. His tan shirt was embroidered with an eagle. He looked too sleek without his machete and knife, quite too scrubbed, although some fine charcoal dust still lodged in his ears.

María helped out Mamacita, her mother-in-law, who puffed and blew her way in grinning amiably from ear to ear. María had on a white bride's gown and veil, her funny legs were wholly covered, and her face was like a brown raisin floating in milk.

I scolded them roundly for spending their money on such clothes.

"*Sí,* señor," they agreed politely, not arguing, and looked at each other happily.

"Where are your donkeys, Don Gabriel? It isn't a fiesta without them."

"And how could I bring donkeys in the car you sent, even if the chauffeur would permit such a thing?"

"Anyway, my new chayote vine will suffer less damage. But at least little Diego should be here to bless your wedding."

"I gave him an extra pile of zacate and put a new ribbon

in his ears," said María, "and I'll take him a tidbit from here."

The mariachi orchestra struck up "*Mi Amorcito*," My Little Love.

"Music, too." María clasped her hands. "You are too good to us."

"It's the orchestra Don Aurelio likes. He provided it, not I."

Rosalinda closed up her shop to come early. Castanets, lovely and lively and burning softly, came with Antonio and Marta. Most of my best friends were there. We danced the rest of the afternoon away. Mario sat on a box in a corner or beamed but presently crouched on his haunches beside the mariachi players. Now and then Petra yanked him out of reverie to send him flying on some last-minute errand.

"Happy these days, Lupe?" I asked, as she snuggled to me in a *danzón*. "When are you going to get married, like María? If you do it quickly, before I leave, I'll throw you a party, too."

"Who would marry *me?*" she scoffed, this pretty one of the family.

"Who wouldn't?"

She pressed closer. "But the fourteen candles. That's a long time yet."

"We'll get you another cake, and I'll help you blow them all out this time. That would change your luck."

"Ah, there's no one just now. I always fall for worthless scamps who would never make good husbands. But señor, they know better how to love."

The mariachi played on tirelessly. Petra kept them well supplied with drinks. After dark, Gabriel, the night watchman, passing by on his rounds, stopped in, smiling, every hour and also had a drink. His good-wishes and his "All's well" whistle grew more birdlike and fanciful as the night wore on.

But it was Castanets I loved dancing with, her red hair against my cheek. Nobody danced better than Castanets. She was sweet tonight and very gay, yet an unusual silence in her because I would soon be leaving.

Father Xavier came in puffing and beaming, an Indian wide of girth, a good man who worked hard with his people and was adored by all. He downed a tequila rather than the punch and, after the ceremony, his unusual appetite threatened to leave all the other guests foodless. His gusto over the food made Petra breathless with happiness.

The time had come. Padre Xavier had on his golden chasuble, book in hand. Gabriel and María were happy and frightened. Marta was the *madrina* and I the *padrino*.

Hardly had Xavier started than there was a commotion at the door, loud talk, an imperative bang on the big drum. Father Xavier looked up annoyed. Were all Mexican weddings, I wondered, doomed to be interrupted?

In burst José, my lost gardener. But he was more than that to Petra. He was her man, and with a little gesture she took him back, a little nod he could understand, no more, which was her way, the glow in her face told the whole story. But there was a slight purse in her lips, too, which left no doubt there would be a few little accounts to be settled with him when the proper moment came.

José had fortified himself for his homecoming with too many rounds of pulque, and now he confronted Gabriel menacingly, though Gabriel was more than half a head taller. "What is going on here?" he demanded, with a bravado he had never before displayed. "What do you mean, marrying my daughter without my permission?"

"And pray, where have you been all this time?" Petra put

in furiously. "Was he to climb Popocatepetl looking for you?"

"He made no effort," said José, with enormous dignity.

Petra flounced. "Since when did María become your daughter?"

"What is yours, sweet woman, is also mine."

Gabriel was getting angry but did not know what to do. The rigmarole had gone far enough, and I said to José sternly, "Gabriel is a fine man, who will never run away from his wife as some men do. And now you come back, full of pulque."

He wanted to take umbrage but after one look at my face he subsided. "Señor, any man who is good enough for you is good enough for me."

"He's good enough for María, and that's all that matters."

He proceeded to give Gabriel a hearty *abrazo* as his new son-in-law and, in right good spirit, Gabriel thumped him back. "A tequilita, you and I, big man, *hombrón,* that you are."

Father Xavier was getting nettled now, but I winked at him, and he waited patiently, book in hand.

"José," I said sharply, "you have already made too much trouble. The wedding was already started. What you have done is not nice or proper. This is not the time for toasts. What is more, you have neglected my garden."

"*Si,* señor," he said meekly, and moved over beside Petra.

And so the couple were married, and the party went on. Even Father Xavier essayed a few steps with Lupe and Castanets before leaving.

It was long after midnight when Antonio and Marta, who had to open their shop early, started the exodus. As Castanets was putting on her green plaid coat to go with them, she leaned her head against mine. "Kiss me," she said, and suddenly shook with sobs.

"Are you coming?" Marta called.

"Go along, you and Antonio. I'll stay awhile. I'll get home all right."

"I'll see to it," I promised.

All were gone. The mariachi players wearily tucked their instruments under their arms. Petra and José were the last to leave. The party had pretty well trampled the chayote vine out of existence. "You won't have to cut off its head this year," I told Petra.

"I shall do that," said José, "and plant you something worth having." But he knew it wasn't so, for I was soon leaving.

The following week another American artist, wishing to move to Coyoacán, bought my furniture and rented my place. Several weeks later my bags were packed.

María and Gabriel came all the way across the Pedregal, with the donkeys, to bid me good-by, and the chayote vine really was finished. Little Diego, bedecked with ribbons, sat up and prayed for me.

I kissed María. "Treat her nicely, Gabriel. You're a lucky man."

"She's a good enough wife," he said fiercely, whetting his big dangerous knife on his trousers as if he were preparing to carve up the world.

I embraced them all, Mexican style: Petra and Mario and José and pretty Lupe. José bustled my bags into the waiting car. "Lend a hand, Mario. The Señor can't stand around all day. He has to catch the train."

The car bumped over the cobbles. I waved to Rosalinda

out in the sun. But the last person I saw on sleepy Ave María Street in the little town of Red Dogs was Petra, best woman of this world, daubing at her eyes with her *rebozo*. So ended two of the richest, happiest years of my life.